Just over 100 years ago, Charles
church as he profoundly raised t
Now, from the pen of a frontline v
beyond the question and DO the sayings of Jesus. This is a must read for
the 21st century church!

DANNY R. THOMAS, D.H.L., PRESIDENT, GRACE PLACE MINISTRIES

Not just another academic book! Dr. Spillman's book, *Do What Jesus Did*,
is a wonderful change from the typical academic book focused on knowing about Jesus. It is about knowing Christ Jesus and then allowing His
life to be lived out today in the life of every believer. The book is, appro-
priately, both encouraging and convicting. Encouraging, in the revelation
that Jesus is alive and well, actively engaging in ministering His gospel
and kingdom on earth today through the lives of saints willing to follow
obediently where He leads. And convicting, when we think of how much
our personal will and choices limit that life we could experience. I have
added Dr. Spillman's book to my required text for all of my Spiritual For-
mation students.

DR. KENNETH DIETRICH, PRESIDENT, TACOMA BIBLE COLLEGE

I believe God is moving in his people around the world to realize the
fullness of what the gospel means. The Good News of Jesus Christ is not
simply that our sins are forgiven and that we are welcomed into heaven—
as glorious as that part of the message is! The fullness of the gospel means
that we have literally been given a New Creation Nature that is fully and
eternally united with Jesus Christ Himself. This reality of *us in Christ* and
Christ in us by the Spirit has opened a whole new reality for us in terms
of how we can live and act and be like Jesus. Dr. Richard Spillman's *Do
What Jesus Did* is a blessing to the body of Christ to release more of this
Truth. What you learn here will stir you to believe that you can "do all
things through Christ who strengthens you."

GARRETT WALTZ, PASTOR, FREEDOM RIVER OUTREACH, TACOMA WA

incredible...its gold...fire...revelation...real...authentic...transforming...amazing

BRIAN BRENT, PASTOR, NEW SONG CHURCH, TACOMA WA;
INSTRUCTOR, YOUTH WITH A MISSION

DR. RICHARD SPILLMAN

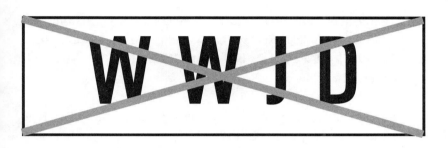

DWJD

WWJD is of no value unless we are willing to Do What Jesus Did.

DEEP RIVER BOOKS
Sisters, Oregon
www.deepriverbooks.com

ISBN-13: 9781937756826
ISBN-10: 1937756823

Library of Congress: 2013935021

Cover design by David Litwin, Purefusion Media

DEDICATION

I dedicate this book to those who taught me what it means to do what Jesus did:

Brian Brent, who taught me to pray like Jesus.
Bonnie Spillman, who taught me to love like Jesus.
Michelle Sweem, who taught me to serve and encourage others like Jesus.
Brent Eriksen, who taught me to forgive like Jesus.
Jon Graciano, who taught me to be humble like Jesus.
Ben Windham, who taught me to walk in power like Jesus.
And Freedom River Outreach church, where everyone's goal is to be like Jesus.

Contents

PREFACE

I still remember sitting in a middle school assembly on great men and women in history. I wasn't paying a lot of attention; I thought having a break from classes was the most interesting part of the whole ordeal. That is, until the subject of Albert Einstein came up. Perhaps it was when the speaker said "He saw the world in a different and new way" that my ears perked up. I had always been kind of shy and a loner. *Maybe that's what's different about me,* I thought. Maybe, like Einstein, I saw the world in a different way and as a result didn't fit in. The whole idea intrigued me. I started to listen. I sat there mesmerized as I heard about the strange and wonderful way Einstein saw things. It changed my life, because then and there I decided I wanted to be like him.

I went home and told my mother that when I grew up, I wanted to win the Nobel Prize like Einstein. He became the first real role model in my life. He influenced my choice of profession, my commitment to study in school, what I read, and how I saw the world. The whole direction of my life changed because of that one decision. I didn't know it at the time, but years later, a new role model was to come into my life—one who would make an even greater difference.

Like Einstein was for me, role models are an important part of our growth process. They teach us acceptable behavior. They define our goals and aspirations. They show us how to overcome obstacles. They inspire us to reach our full potential. They change our perspective on the world. We imitate their behaviors, respect their opinions, and even adopt their moral codes.

Who we choose as our role model defines who we become. It certainly did for me. As such, choosing a role model is one of the most important decisions we will make.

The New Testament author of Hebrews understood this principle as he urged believers to find good role models: "Imitate those who through faith and patience inherit what has been promised" (Hebrews 6:12). Paul understood this when he asked the Corinthian church to imitate him (1 Corinthians 4:16). For Christians, though, the ultimate role model is Jesus. That's who Paul really wanted all of us to imitate. He told the church at Ephesus, "Be imitators of God, therefore, as dearly loved children and live a life of love, just as Christ loved us" (Ephesians 5:1–2).

Jesus as our role model is not a difficult sell, because all believers long to connect with Jesus in some way, to share some part of him. Some want the heart of Jesus so they can know what it means to truly love. Some want the eyes of Jesus so they can see others as he sees them. Some want the wisdom of Jesus so they can know truth. Some want the feet of Jesus so they can walk the path of a servant. In fact, we are described in 1 Corinthians 2:16 as already having "the mind of Christ." Yet, the reality is we are called to even more. We are called to be all that Jesus was—to imitate everything about his life and to do what he did. Paul praised the Thessalonian church for doing just that in 1 Thessalonians 1:6, where he wrote, "You became imitators of us and of the Lord."

The apostle John made this calling clear in 3 John 11: "Do not imitate what is evil but what is good. Anyone who does what is good is from God." Imitating Jesus *is* imitating the things of God. All that Jesus was, we are called to be.

Imitating Jesus is far more than accepting him into your heart. In fact, the common description of becoming a Christian, "accepting Jesus into your heart," never appears in the Bible. Our "being in Christ" is a far more accurate description of salvation than Christ's being in us. Salvation is not so much the result of Jesus's coming into our lives as it is the impact of our entering into the life of Christ. The truth is, Jesus didn't come just so he could live inside us. He came so our lives would embody his. Jesus does not want to be hidden away in our hearts; he wants us to be in him, to be like him in every way. He came to be our ultimate role model. What he did is what we are to do. How he lived is how we are to live.

The purpose of this book is to explore what it means to do what Jesus did. It is to answer what may very well be the most important questions we could ever ask. How can we be like Jesus? Exactly how can we do what Jesus did while he was on earth? What did he do that was so different? Why is it so difficult to follow his path? How can we make his life and his choices into our lives and our choices?

Being like Jesus is a tall order, requiring a special commitment, but it is the ultimate fulfillment of the gospel. It begins with an encounter with Jesus. We must know him before we can become like him. So in some ways, this book is more than just an examination of what Jesus did. It is an introduction to the one who gave his all so we could be everything God designed us to be. It is not a book about simply knowing what Jesus would do. Rather, it is about being so surrendered to him, so much a part of him, that we *do* what he would do. It is a call to a new life—to become the new creature Paul talked about. It is a biography, but not one that looks at the life of Jesus over time. It is a study of the qualities of his life that we should admire and imitate.

Doing what Jesus did is a great adventure, one in which you will be called to deny yourself (Luke 9:23), yet one in which your burden will be light (Matthew 11:30). You will be asked to surrender your life as you see it so you can find it as he lived it (Matthew 16:25). My prayer is that this book will be the catalyst for change, that it will awaken the new creature inside you and release the life that God has planned for you all along. I pray that you will choose Jesus Christ as your role model and that every aspect of your life will follow his example.

Chapter One

JESUS CAN BE YOUR ROLE MODEL

I spent the first thirty years after I became a Christian pursuing the wrong goal. I attended church. I prayed, sometimes. I read and periodically studied my Bible. As I grew as a Christian, I taught an occasional adult Sunday school class and became a popular teacher at church. Eventually, I taught Sunday school six months every year, alternating quarters with my pastor. I was even asked from time to time to preach in his place. Even though I never led anyone to Christ, I thought nothing of it because I was teaching others about Christ. At no time was I doing anything wrong—I just stopped short of doing things completely right. As a result, I was missing out on the greatest adventure of my life, and what was worse, I didn't even know it.

My Christian life was like the jewelry so popular a few years ago that had the letters "WWJD" on it—"What Would Jesus Do?" From my study of the Bible, I knew exactly what Jesus would do. I taught others what Jesus would do. I could quote chapter and verse about what Jesus would do. But that was as far as I went.

I thought my life was complete, but it was empty and void of purpose. I studied the life of Jesus like I might have studied the life of Einstein or someone else I admired when I should have been studying his life so I could learn to be like him. At the time, I didn't realize that asking "What would Jesus do?" was of no value unless I was willing to *do* what Jesus did. Robert Odom once wrote in a Love INC newsletter, "There is no shortage of people talking about Christ, there is a shortage of people living like Christ." That was me: all talk, no action.

I now realize the popular jewelry should have read "DWJD," or "Do What Jesus Did." I came to that realization after my daughter took me to a new church. While it took some time to realize what was going on, there was clearly something different about this place. It was a tough time in my life. I had just lost my first grandson, and his death had hit me hard. I questioned everything in my life, including my position with God. Then I walked into New Song for the first time. The worship service had already begun, and it was loud. Not in an abusive way, but in a celebratory way. It was a party. For the first time in weeks, I felt joy. It felt like a fresh wind blowing over my face. It was both refreshing and uplifting. In minutes, I was in tears. Like a lost sheep, I had been found. I had come home. The pain didn't go away, but I left that evening knowing my life was about to change.

After several weeks, I had healed enough to begin to take in the messages. Instead of intellectual Bible studies such as the ones I had been leading for so many years, the pastor talked in more practical terms about who Jesus was and what he did. He called his teaching "Jesus Ministry." It was all about walking in Jesus's footsteps, doing what he did. For this church, it was not enough to study the Bible to discover Jesus. They studied the Bible to become like him.

The biggest change came the night I went forward for prayer after the service. New Song always ended with an altar call, but not the traditional "Come forward if you want to accept Jesus." That night, Pastor Brian, as usual, called the prayer teams forward and then said, "If you are seeking God's plan for your life and need prayer, don't leave without sitting down with one of these teams."

I had heard that invitation repeated each Saturday night for several weeks. It was a call to discover what New Song called our "spiritual DNA"—the reason why God had put us on this earth. As I sat there near the back expecting to hear the standard invitation, in my mind it was as if the whole church suddenly went empty and dark. The only light was between me and Pastor Brian as he appeared to turn and look me in the eye and say, "Rick, it's time for you to discover God's will for your life." I was shocked. I looked around as I thought, *Did anyone else hear that?*

In a daze, I walked up to the front. I was assigned to a prayer team, and to this day I cannot tell you who they were even though I have since come to know most of the members of New Song. As they prayed with me, I could hear God speaking through them. Somehow they knew why I was at New Song and what I needed. More importantly, I realized that God had never abandoned me. He had been waiting for me to discover my real purpose in life.

I left that night, just as I had left that middle school assembly so many years ago, with a new role model. Jesus went from being an intellectual exercise to being a way of life. I no longer asked, "What would Jesus do in this situation?", satisfied with only the answer. I started to *do* what I thought Jesus would do. For the first time, I understood the command in James 1:22: "Do not merely listen to the word, and so deceive yourselves. *Do what it says.*" I had been deceived all my life. I had only listened to and studied the Word. Now I was ready to start over and do what the Word said.

After all, Jesus did not spend his time asking what the Father would do. Instead, he did what he saw the Father doing. If I was going to imitate Jesus, then I had to start doing the same.

From my study of the Bible, I was aware of the commands Jesus had given, but now I understood that Jesus's entire life was a command. He lived as an example of what our lives should be like. His life was not a suggestion. It was not an illustration of what we could be. His life was a model of what we *should* be. We are expected to follow him. When Jesus told one of his disciples to "Follow me" in Matthew 8:22, the word he used for "follow" really means "to be the same as." In other words, the call to follow Jesus is not a call to stand in line behind him and watch him work; it is a call to walk alongside him, doing what he is doing.

I did not enter into a salvation-by-works mode. I didn't want to do what Jesus did so I could be saved. By faith, I had been saved for more than thirty years. Salvation is a free gift from God. But salvation is not an end; it is a beginning. The "good race" Paul talks about in Galatians 5:7 is not toward salvation, it is toward the realization of a life *in* Christ. For all those years, I had been stuck at the starting line. Finally, I wanted to do what Jesus did *because* I was saved. His blood alone had saved me. Now, his love drove me to want to be like him. The truth is, works do not save, but no one gets saved unless someone works.

The Purpose of His Life

Once I made the commitment to live like Jesus, to do what Jesus did, I launched out on the greatest adventure of my life. It began as I tried to understand the purpose behind Jesus's life. If I was to succeed in doing what Jesus did, I needed to encounter him in a new way. I needed to look at his life not because I wanted to *know* what he did, but so I could *do* what he did.

There were some things I had always known about Jesus. I learned in Sunday school that he came to die for me. But if the only purpose of his coming was to die for our sins, why did he have to spend thirty-three years on earth? Was his life just a precursor to his ultimate purpose? If all that was required was his death, followed by his resurrection three days later, then what was the reason for his three-year ministry? These may seem like strange questions to ask, but by asking them I discovered I had long overlooked the fact that Jesus's life was as important as his death. He came to live as much as he came to die.

Jesus came to show us how to live in the shadow of death, to be constantly tempted by sin, yet never to fear evil. So it follows that it is our responsibility both to accept his gift of salvation and to live by the model he set. We are called to continue the work he began on earth. We are called to live like Jesus in every respect because the purpose of his life was to teach us how to do just that until he returns.

Overall, Jesus had three purposes for coming. He died to pay the price for our sin, so we should accept him. He rose again to claim what he purchased, so we should flock to him. And he lived to teach us how to live, so we should imitate his life.

Can We Live Like Jesus?

Once I understood the purpose of Jesus's life, I had another hurdle to overcome. I needed to know if I actually *could* live like he did. Growing up, no one ever told me that I could never match my then–role model, Albert Einstein. When I announced to my mother, "One day I am going to win the Noble Prize in physics," her response was not, "I love you, but that is way out of your league." Instead, she encouraged me to work at it. Once, I even overheard her bragging to a friend that I would win the Nobel Prize. I am not now and never have been an Albert Einstein, but that is not the issue. By trying to be like him I shaped my life, my career, and my relationships in a positive way.

Unfortunately, too many people—including many within the church—will tell you that you cannot be like Jesus. Do not listen to them, because the Word of God tells you not only to try, but that you can succeed. Just as my mother bragged to a friend about my goal, I believe Jesus is bragging to the Father, "Look at my friend! He wants to be just like me. Isn't that great?"

Once I reached the point of accepting that I could be like Jesus (relying on the same childlike faith that led me to seek to be like Einstein), I had to decide *how* I could be like Jesus. One thing I did know was that living like Jesus required more than living a good life, though the two are often spoken of interchangeably. Most people will tell you they live a good life: "Of course, I don't steal, I have never killed anyone, and I haven't broken any major laws." But not doing wrong things is not enough.

Living like Jesus is fundamentally different from just living a good life. Jesus did not just avoid sin. He battled it; he took authority over it. He lived a life that defined love, compassion, prayer, forgiveness, and grace. He lived a life of confidence, power, and authority.

I could possibly avoid the bad things that Jesus didn't do, but how could I do the good, especially the supernatural things Jesus did? After all, Jesus is God, and that changes everything. On his human side, Jesus experienced what it means to grow up, to feel pain and loss, to know the pull of temptation; but on his God side, Jesus had wisdom, insight, power, and authority that ranged into the realm of the supernatural. While I could appreciate his human side, I could only hope to loosely approximate his God side.

Paul anticipated we would question our ability to act like Jesus, so he wrote this in Philippians 2:5–6: "Your attitude should be the same as that of Christ Jesus: who, being in very nature God, did not consider equality with God something to be grasped." Even though I had read this many times before, in the back of my mind I couldn't help thinking, *Yes, but he still is God. He could do things that I could never do.*

What I always missed was the next verse, where Paul says something far more remarkable: "But [he] made himself nothing." The word for "nothing" literally means "empty." Jesus did more than choose not to carry his God nature to earth; he emptied himself of everything that made him God. He totally separated himself from any special advantage his God nature might have given him.

In a small way, it is similar to when the president of the US assumes office—he has to put all his finances in a blind trust. He can't manage them or even know how they are doing in order to avoid the possibility that he might profit from his decisions as president. Jesus had to put everything that made him God into a blind trust. He could not access them or rely on them in any way to avoid the possibility that anything he would do on earth was related to his position as God. As a result, I could no longer look at the things Jesus did on earth and claim I could not do the same. *He never relied on anything that is not also available to all of us.* Besides, if we can't live like Jesus did, then what is the use of asking what Jesus would do? How is knowing what Jesus would do any help if we cannot do it ourselves?

It is an insidious, terrible lie of Satan that we cannot live as Jesus did. It is a lie designed to hide the truth of his life from us. It is a lie that we can't have as close a relationship with the Father as Jesus did, that we cannot expect to know the will of the Father as Jesus did, that we cannot be used by the Holy Spirit to perform signs and wonders as Jesus did. The enemy is desperate for you to believe this lie because it is the only way he can maintain his authority. An earth populated by redeemed people who are living like Christ is his worst nightmare! He wants to rob us of our destiny at any cost. The sad fact is he has been largely successful, but that can change if we seek to live the life Jesus called us to live.

We can do what Jesus did. Jesus told us so himself in an amazing statement recorded in John 14:12: "I tell you the truth, anyone who has faith in me will do what I have been doing. He will do even greater things than these, because I am going to the Father." Jesus knew this would be hard for us to believe. To drive the point home, he began with "I tell you the truth." In the original, the phrase means "verily, verily"; a better translation would be "surely" or "this is trustworthy." He said it not once, but twice. He wanted us to believe him when he said we could do what he did. It's as if he turned to his disciples and said, "When you hear what I am about to say, you will think I've gone crazy, but I haven't. You will think I must be kidding, but I'm not. You will think that I am lying, but *read my lips:* you can do what I have been doing."

Not only did Jesus stress that what he said was true, his statement was not that we *can* do what he did, but that we *will* do what he did. John 14:12 is not an observation of what we are capable of doing, it is statement of what faith leads us to actually do. Nothing Jesus did, no sign, no wonder, no miracle occurred because he was God. Everything he did occurred because he was a human filled with the Holy Spirit. And as a human also filled with the Spirit, I can do the same.

The Saturday evening I went forward for prayer at New Song, I left with a new and deeper realization of my purpose in life. Even though I had taught the Word for more than thirty years, I was no better than those Jesus described in Matthew 13:13: "Though seeing they do not see; though hearing, they do not hear or understand." All my life I had seen, yet I had been blind to the truth; I had heard but had been deaf to the real meaning of the Word. I had fallen prey to Satan's lies for so long that I had missed the truth that something significant happens when we accept Christ. Our acknowledgment that Jesus paid the price for our sin is important. We can rejoice because at the moment of salvation, we enter into the kingdom. We can look forward to an eternity with the Father. Our future is assured. But something else important happens in the here and now. *We become a new creature.* The emphasis here is on *new.* In spite of seeing it written in God's Word and hearing it taught, I had never stopped to consider what that meant in my life. I was saved, but what was this new creature I had become?

Paul talked a lot about the process of becoming a new creation in Christ. In 2 Corinthians 5:17 he wrote, "Therefore, if anyone is in Christ, he is a new creation; the old has gone, the new has come!" This is not an assurance of something that will happen in the future. Paul did not say that someday the old will be gone and eventually the new will come. The new creation is immediate and real.

Does this new creation manifest itself in everyone's life? Unfortunately, it does not. We are a new creation, but we have to recognize it in ourselves. This is why the lie that we cannot be like Christ is so effective. We are a new creation, but the enemy does not want us to understand what that means. Satan does everything in his power to suppress and hide what we have become.

In an effort to counter the lies of the enemy, Paul explained our new nature in Ephesians 4:22–24: "You were taught, with regard to your former way of life, to put off your old self, which is being corrupted by its deceitful desires; to be made new in the attitude of your minds; and to put on the new self, created to be *like God* in true righteousness and holiness."

This was such an important concept that Paul wrote about it not only to the churches at Ephesus and Corinth but also to the Colossian church: "Do not lie to each other, since you have taken off your old self with its practices and have put on the new self, which is being renewed in knowledge in the image of its Creator" (Colossians 3:9–10). We are all called to take off the old and put on the new. Most believers take off the old, but all too few put on the new. Realizing that this requires our active participation, Satan uses lies to discourage us from becoming what we are in Christ. He certainly does not want us to "put on the new self" or live "in the image of [our] Creator."

I now understand what that new creature is—it is the very likeness of Jesus. This is exactly what Paul described in 2 Corinthians 3:18: "And we, who with unveiled faces all reflect the Lord's glory, *are being transformed into his likeness* with ever-increasing glory, which comes from the Lord, who is the Spirit."

It couldn't be any clearer than the way Paul explained it in Galatians 3:26–27: "You are all sons of God through faith in Christ Jesus, for all of you who were baptized into Christ have *clothed yourselves with Christ.*" In

Greek, the phrase "clothed yourselves with Christ" is even more powerful than it sounds in English. It means to put on the person and character of Christ. That is your new creature. This is why Peter wrote in 1 Peter 2:21, "To this you were called, because Christ suffered for you, leaving you *an example* that you *should* follow in his steps." The word translated "example" literally means "a copy for imitation."

YOU CAN DO WHAT JESUS DID

Can we really live like Jesus? My answer is an emphatic, unquestionable yes! No less an authority than Jesus himself told us so. Paul wrote at length to the Galatians, the Corinthians, the Colossians, and the Ephesians exhorting them to do so. The issue is not *can we,* but *how* do we live like Jesus?

Paul told us how. "Let the Holy Spirit guide your lives. Then you won't be doing what your sinful nature craves" (Galatians 5:16, NLT). Living like Jesus was the goal for Paul. He described the mature Christian to the Ephesians as "attaining to the whole measure of the fullness of Christ" (Ephesians 4:13). It is probably the case that John understood what Jesus was saying in John 14:12, that we would do the same things Jesus did, better than anyone. Not only did he record that specific teaching of Jesus, but he later made the point in 1 John 4:17 that *"As he is, so are we* in this world."

The truth is that we already *are* new creatures. We *are* the likeness of Christ. We are filled with the Holy Spirit for a reason, and it is not so we can just talk about Jesus! We are here to show others the real Jesus. We are to be much more than conveyers of information about Jesus. We are called to be walking illustrations of him. The world doesn't need another person saying, "Do you know Jesus?" It needs someone who will say, "Watch, this is what Jesus did."

Chapter Two

PRAY LIKE JESUS PRAYED

It was late at night as I knelt down by my daughter's bed. As I had done for the last several months, I cried out to God for healing. I commanded the enemy to leave her alone. I pleaded for God to protect her. I was facing the greatest challenge in any father's life, and it was quickly becoming more than I could bear.

My young daughter, Annie, was suffering from a serious, life-threatening illness. She had been in and out of hospitals, but all the doctors could do was adjust her medication to try to control her disease. There was no hope of a cure. I was told that 25 percent of children with this illness died before age twenty-four.

Throughout her illness, I felt helpless. There seemed to be nothing I could do to make her better. I did not understand what she was going through or how to respond to her needs. I could not sleep at night. I woke at two or three in the morning and simply could not get back to sleep. I began to get angry at God. I was frustrated by my sleepless nights. I searched for something positive that I could do.

Eventually, I decided to use this time to pray for Annie. I went up to her room and knelt over her bed. I put one hand on her and prayed for God to protect her. I had done this for months, but one night, something different happened. As I got up to leave, I heard a little voice say, "I love you, Daddy." It melted my heart.

Neither of us mentioned that prayer time the next morning. I had no idea that this ritual of prayer would continue for four years. Every night I would slip into her room, and two or three times a week, as I left, I would hear, "I love you, Daddy."

I am happy to report that ten years later, Annie is completely healed and doing very well. She is married, has two beautiful children, and is walking with the Lord. During her ordeal, I discovered two things about prayer. First, it is powerful. And second, before those four years, I didn't understand it at all.

My four-year experience taught me that any discussion of how Jesus lived has to begin with the subject of prayer. Any instruction on how to model the life of Jesus must start with prayer. In any situation in which we might ask the question, "What would Jesus do?", the first answer should always be that he would pray. Hence, doing what Jesus did means we should find ourselves in prayer. A lot.

Of course this should be obvious from even the most casual examination of the life of Christ. He never did anything without prayer. John 9:12 tells us that before he selected the twelve apostles, he spent the night in prayer. He taught us in the parable of the judge, found in Luke 18:1–6, that we should always pray and never stop. Paul later wrote to the Colossian church and instructed them to "devote yourself to prayer" (Colossians 4:2). I certainly learned that lesson praying for my daughter. If I am to do what Jesus did, I should never do anything without first praying.

But Jesus's prayer life was different, not just in quantity but in quality as well. Even the apostles recognized that. So how do we pray like he did? The answer begins with an understanding of prayer itself.

WHAT IS PRAYER?

I would venture a guess that almost everyone prays at one time or another. Dr Rodney Stark, a Baylor University professor of sociology, noted that "Prayer is one of the most common and unacknowledged activities on the planet." A survey by the National Institutes of Health discovered that 43 percent of all adults prayed for their health in 2003. An informal survey of 79,000 people from all faiths around the world found that over 72 percent had prayed during their lifetimes. All around the United States, children kneel at their bedsides, reciting the words, "Now I lay me down to sleep . . ." Families around the world bow their heads over the dinner table and offer thanks. Every Sunday, churches are filled with praying people. Pagans pray to their gods. Muslims bow in prayer, facing

Mecca, five times a day. Even atheists are prone to pray in moments of extreme crisis. The world is filled with prayer beads, prayer rugs, prayer wheels, prayer bowls, prayer candles, and prayer flags. There is a world-wide prayer industry. Something in our nature cries out to pray. But the question remains: "What is prayer?"

It is hard to accept that something so simple, so widely practiced, so much a part of the human experience can be so misunderstood. My best summary of the mystery of prayer is this: praying is easy, talking to God is hard.

For most people, praying is easy because it is defined by a set of rules. The rules specify when it is best to pray, how to start a prayer, how to end a prayer, what is acceptable to say in prayer, and what you should do while praying. Prayers are given before meals, in church, or when you are in distress. Prayers begin with "Dear Jesus" or "Our Father" or some variation on that theme. Prayers end with "Amen." Prayers contain praise and requests. Prayers are offered in a reverent manner with eyes closed and heads bowed. If you can't think of something to say, you read a prayer someone else has written or finger some beads or hold a prayer cloth. These rules make it easy to know how to pray without having to understand prayer.

The truth is that prayer is simply talking to God, but talking to God is hard because there are no rules. You might think the lack of rules would make it easier, but we are actually more comfortable when rules define our behavior. Without rules, we don't know what is right and what is wrong. Regarding something as important as prayer, we want guidelines. We want to do it right so we can get an answer.

And therein lies the fundamental problem. Our goal for prayer is al-most always seeking some form of answer, but prayer is not about an-swers from God—prayer is about connecting *with* God. When Jesus prayed, it was a means to remain connected to God so he could know what the Father was doing and do the same thing himself. He didn't seek answers to prayer; he sought direction through prayer.

Ultimately, prayer is simple. Strip away all the religious stuff, and prayer is nothing more than talking to God as one friend to another.

Which, when you think about it, is so much more than what we often practice when we pray.

Why Is Prayer So Difficult?

Understanding that prayer is the process of talking to God, why has it become so difficult to do it right in spite of the fact that it is done so often? After attending New Song, where everyone seemed to be talking to God during prayer, this was a question I asked about myself. All my Christian life I had been praying, but there have been few times, until recently, when I have really talked to God. I am not alone. It is probably safe to say that almost every Christian prays, but few talk to God.

There are two reasons why talking to God seems so difficult. First, it is not what we have been taught in church—prayer is learned by example rather than by instruction, and our examples are lacking. Second, talking to God as one friend to another implies we have to listen as much as we speak.

Problem One: Prayer Is Learned By Example

It has been my observation while visiting churches over the past thirty years that there is little instruction on prayer. Of course there are Sunday school courses, books, and sermons on the Lord's Prayer, but little is taught on the mechanics of prayer. Why should there be? Everyone prays, so we must all know how. The result is that we learn about prayer by example. You bow your head, close your eyes, start with "Dear Jesus," end with "Amen," and in between you say nice things to God and ask him to solve your problems because that is what everyone else does. If you are really serious, you might get on your knees. If you are truly desperate, you might lie facedown on the ground. None of those things are wrong, but they are too ritualistic. When viewed as the *nature* of prayer instead of as simple trappings, they hinder the process.

A close friend of mine once confessed she had a difficult time praying in church. Whenever she closed her eyes to pray, she found that her mind wandered. She couldn't concentrate. The answer was easy. I told her it was okay to pray with her eyes open. She was shocked. She had never considered it! In her mind, the mechanics of prayer were fixed. Prayer required her eyes be closed. Later, she told me that after a few Sundays of praying with her eyes open, her prayer time became more powerful than it had ever been.

PROBLEM TWO: PRAYER IS NOT APPROACHED AS A CONVERSATION

There is something different about talking to God, about being in his presence and letting out everything we feel, that makes just talking to God more difficult than "praying" to God. What makes it most difficult is that talking to God is a conversation, not a soliloquy. Our examples of prayer are skewed because we only hear one side of what is supposed to be a conversation.

As a result, the church, by and large, has an unbalanced view of prayer. We may claim that prayer is a conversation with God, but in practice, we do all the talking. Think about your own experience. How many times in church have you been asked to bow your head and pray (read "speak") to God? Contrast that with the number of times you have been told to quietly sit and listen to God. If your experience is anything like mine, the number of times you have been asked to speak to God vastly outnumber the times you have been asked to listen. Yet what we have to say is the least important part of prayer! Jesus tells us God already knows what we need before we ask (Matthew 6:8). Hence, the most important part of this conversation that we call prayer is not what we have to say, but what God has to say. That means prayer is mainly a time for us to listen to God—yet we rarely do that.

But God wants us to listen to him. When Peter declared that Jesus was "the Son of the living God" in Matthew 16:16, he said this not because he knew it naturally, but because he had listened to God reveal the truth. Jesus acknowledged this in the next verse: "This was not revealed to you by man, but by my Father in heaven." Jesus made it clear that we are to listen just as Peter did when he declared, "My sheep *listen to my voice;* I know them, and they follow me" (John 10:27).

What must have stood out to the disciples was that Jesus walked away from prayer with something they had never seen before. Jesus didn't make a request of God and then wait for some event to occur that confirmed God had heard the prayer. Jesus came away from prayer with something immediate, a level of confidence and a certainty that he knew what to do next, because he had heard from God during prayer. Jesus didn't just talk to God; he listened to God. Jesus prayed so he could learn what his Father wanted from him more than he did to motivate the Father to do something for him. He said as much in John 5:19. When Jesus was confronted in the temple, he said, "[The Son] can do only what he sees his Father doing, because whatever the Father does the Son also does." Jesus rarely asked God to do things for him. He mainly asked God to give him things to do.

I wish I could say I have practiced this most of my Christian life, but for more than three decades, my prayers involved me more than God. The first day I visited New Song, I was told that God wanted to talk to me, and it rocked my world. For me, this was a revolutionary concept. It meant that my prayers had to become a means to building a relationship with God. Prayer was not a time for me to call God to action. Rather, prayer was a time for God to call me to act. I needed to listen. Evidently God has a voice, and he uses it.

This was not only revolutionary to me, it was borderline heresy in the church I was regularly attending. The elders in my home church told me in no uncertain terms that God does not speak to us in anything more than perhaps vague impressions. I was told to stop talking about what I had heard from God. At the time I was hurt, confused, and sad, but now I know their reaction came out of their fear. The elders were fearful that I might hear God incorrectly, and it would cause serious problems. Yet, our fear should not be, "What if I hear God incorrectly?" It should be, "What if I don't hear God at all?"

To this day, I don't know how I missed this point most of my Christian life. God's desire to speak to all of us is an important biblical principle. In the Old Testament, God constantly complained that no one would listen to him. Jeremiah 6:10 is one of many verses highlighting God's frustration: "To whom can I speak and give warning? Who will listen to me? Their ears are closed so they cannot hear. The Word of the

Lord is offensive to them; they find no pleasure in it."

Even more frightening is what God said in Zechariah 7:11–13: "But they refused to pay attention; stubbornly they turned their backs and stopped up their ears. They made their hearts as hard as flint and would not listen. So the LORD Almighty was very angry. 'When I called, they did not listen; so when they called, I would not listen,' says the LORD Almighty." God's response to those stubborn people, who over and over again refused to listen to him, was to stop listening to them. Praise God that he is patient, or he would have stopped listening to me a long time ago!

Jesus told us in John 16:12–15 that one of the purposes of the Holy Spirit was to guide us in modeling his life, and that meant listening to what he had to say:

> I still have many things to say to you, but you cannot bear them now. However, when He, the Spirit of truth, has come, He will guide you into all truth; for He will not speak on His own authority, but whatever He hears He will speak; and He will tell you things to come. He will glorify Me, for He will take of what is Mine and declare it to you. All things that the Father has are Mine. Therefore I said that He will take of Mine and declare it to you. (NKJV)

Notice Jesus tells us he has many more things to say to us, but he will tell the Holy Spirit, who will then tell us. Thus, as well as reading and studying the Word of God, we are also to listen to what the Holy Spirit has to tell us, just as Christ listened to the Father.

Paul made this clear when he wrote to the Romans, "So faith comes by hearing and hearing by the Word of God" (Romans 10:17). I always thought this verse meant that someone would read the Bible out loud, and those listening would gain faith. This is certainly reasonable, and it is one of the ways we can grow in faith, but it is not what Paul means here. In this verse, the word used for "Word" is *Rhema*, which means "hearing the voice," rather than *Logos,* which means "recorded word" and is often used to indicate the Bible. A better translation of Romans 10:17 would be, "So faith comes by hearing and hearing *by listening to the voice of God.*"

None of this devalues the written Word of God. Even though we are to listen to God, the Bible remains as important as ever. It serves as our study guide, our doorway into God's heart, and a means of testing what we hear to verify it is from God.

Charles Spurgeon emphasized this in *The Check Book of the Bank of Faith:*

> Note well that we must hear Jesus speak if we expect Him to hear us speak. If we have no ear for Christ, He will have no ear for us. In proportion as we hear we shall be heard. Moreover, what is heard must remain, must live in us, and must abide in our character as a force and a power. We must receive the truths which Jesus taught, the precepts which He issued, and the movements of His Spirit within us; or we shall have no power at the Mercy Seat.

When I made the commitment to listen to God as well as talk to him, things started happening in my life. I discovered that God was speaking to me, not in an audible voice, but in subtle ways that became quite clear. I started to take risks, and God began to reveal himself in amazing ways.

For example, one day during prayer God told me to go to the Nativity House, a place where homeless people hang out during the week in Tacoma. I was to look for a man in a white dress shirt named Ron. Ron needed prayer, and God said he was sending me to pray for him. I had some time after lunch, so I drove over. As soon as I entered, I saw a tall man across the room at the phone; he was the only one in the building wearing a white dress shirt. I walked over and stood by him. As soon as he hung up the phone, I asked if by any chance his name was Ron.

"No," he replied, "it's John."

Everything in me told me this was the man I was to pray for, so I took a risk. "John, God told me to come here today and look for someone named Ron wearing a white dress shirt just like yours."

He said, "John, Ron, easy mistake."

I breathed a sigh of relief. It didn't look like I was going to make a fool of myself, so I continued. "He sent me to pray for you. Do you need prayer, by any chance?"

Then John told me his story. "Yes, I do. In fact, when I got up this morning I said, 'God, I need someone to pray for me.' You see, I just lost my job because I had an accident and cut off the tip of my little finger." He held up his left hand to show me his bandaged finger.

John continued, "I have been on the phone all morning trying to find someone to help me, but nothing is working out. I just need some encouragement, someone to tell me it is going to be okay. That's why I asked God to send someone to pray for me."

I prayed for healing, both for his finger and his situation. As I left, he thanked me and said I had made his day. The truth is, John had made my day!

My wife, Bonnie, had a similar experience early in her growth as a prayer warrior. One afternoon, we were praying for a young lady whom I will call Susan at a conference sponsored by New Song. In the middle of the prayer time, God spoke to Bonnie, telling her that Susan was afraid she had lost her salvation. We had never met her and knew nothing about her. She wasn't from our church and had just decided to attend the conference that afternoon. It took some courage on Bonnie's part to speak up. She paused to think about the consequences of what she was about to ask, but she decided to trust what she believed God was telling her.

Bonnie raised her head from prayer, looked directly at Susan, and asked, "You think you can lose your salvation, don't you?"

Susan had a look of total shock on her face. After a few moments of silence, she started to cry. "Yes," she admitted through the tears, "I'm afraid that I could mess up and lose everything. But how did you know?"

"Why do you feel that way?" Bonnie asked.

That's when Susan opened up and told us her story. "I moved to Tacoma about a year ago. At my church in California, I discovered I had a gift of ministering to women. I began working with women in my church, and after a while I was helping women all through my community. I never thought I could lose my salvation. But when I moved here and found a new church, I was taught that salvation was not guaranteed. I could lose it if I stepped out of line. At first I struggled with the idea, but everyone in my new church accepted it. I began to be scared. I kept asking myself, 'Am I really saved?' I didn't have the heart to start ministering to women again. All my energy went into constantly judging myself, finding myself unworthy of serving others, always praying, asking God to save me. I hate what I have become and miss working with women."

We spent the rest of the prayer time assuring her from the Word that she was saved. At the end, she thanked us and told us she was excited to once again serve others in the name of Jesus. If Bonnie had not listened to God and acted on what she heard, this young lady would have left in an entirely different state of mind.

Listening to the Father and doing what he says is the greatest feeling in the world. There is nothing like it. But we have to start looking at prayer as a conversation and listen to God as much or more than we speak to him.

How Did Jesus Pray?

Jesus prayed in a way that was noticeably different. His disciples saw it, and they were prompted to ask, "Lord, teach us to pray, just as John taught his disciples" (Luke 11:1). Prayer was an important part of Jewish life. The disciples had certainly prayed many times. They had seen and heard the prayers of religious leaders of the time. They were familiar with the concept of prayer, but Jesus went about it in a different way—a way so different they felt they needed to be taught all over again. They realized they couldn't learn to pray like Jesus just by copying him.

So Jesus taught them. His radically different approach to prayer was easy to follow once they understood that prayer was talking with God. His teaching is found in Matthew 6:1–16:

Be careful not to do your "acts of righteousness" before men, to be seen by them. If you do, you will have no reward from your Father in heaven. So when you give to the needy, do not announce it with trumpets, as the hypocrites do in the synagogues and on the streets, to be honored by men. I tell you the truth, they have received their reward in full. But when you give to the needy, do not let your left hand know what your right hand is doing, so that your giving may be in secret. Then your Father, who sees what is done in secret, will reward you. And when you pray, do not be like the hypocrites, for they love to pray standing in the synagogues and on the street corners to be seen by men. I tell you the truth, they have received their reward in full. But when you pray, go into your room, close the door and pray to your Father, who is unseen. Then your Father, who sees what is done in secret, will reward you. And when you pray, do not keep on babbling like pagans, for they think they will be heard because of their many words. Do not be like them, for your Father knows what you need before you ask him. This, then, is how you should pray:

"Our Father in heaven,
hallowed be your name,
your kingdom come,
your will be done
on earth as it is in heaven.
Give us today our daily bread.
Forgive us our debts,
as we also have forgiven our debtors.
And lead us not into temptation,
but deliver us from the evil one."

For if you forgive men when they sin against you, your heavenly Father will also forgive you. But if you do not forgive men their sins, your Father will not forgive your sins. When you fast, do not look somber as the hypocrites do, for they disfigure their faces to show men they are fasting. I tell you the truth, they have received their reward in full.

In his teaching, Jesus made several principles of prayer clear. Those principles are key in understanding how to pray like Jesus prayed.

PRINCIPLE 1: PRAYER IS AN "ACT OF RIGHTEOUSNESS"

Jesus began his instruction on prayer by identifying three acts of righteousness: helping the needy (Matthew 6:2), praying (Matthew 6:5), and fasting (Matthew 6:16). Before I studied these verses, I had never thought about what it meant to be righteous. Righteousness always seemed to be a label given by God to characterize an entire lifestyle, a lifestyle, I might add, that seemed way beyond my grasp. But here Jesus is teaching that prayer is one of the three things that a righteous person does. Jesus practiced all three. As a result, we are called to imitate all three.

So what is the connection between these three actions that raise them to the level of acts of righteousness? Helping the needy is the act of serving God. God said if you do anything for the least of these, you do it for me. Praying is the act of entering into the presence of God. It is a time when we connect with God. Fasting is the act of seeking God, giving up something to make more room for him in our lives.

A righteous person seeks God, serves God, and connects with God. Prayer is more than a time to mouth a few words with your eyes closed or to ask God's blessing before a meal. Prayer is the righteous act of entering into the presence of God. No one can pray like Jesus did without understanding the enormous implications of performing what is fundamentally an act of righteousness.

PRINCIPLE 2: IMPRESSING MAN IS NOT THE PURPOSE OF PRAYER

The first thing Jesus emphasized about prayer in Matthew 6:1, and perhaps the first thing that caught the attention of the disciples, was that prayer involves an intimate connection to God. I had never understood the importance of intimacy in prayer until I came across a short verse in the beginning of Genesis 3.

After Adam and Eve sinned, but before God confronted them, Genesis 3:8 gives a brief but powerful picture of life in the garden. It begins with the statement that Adam and Eve heard "the sound of the LORD God walking in the garden in the cool of the day." The fact that God walked in the garden did not surprise Adam and Eve. Evidently, God had walked in the garden with them on many occasions. However, this time, instead of joining him, they hid because they feared his response to their disobedience.

Whenever I read this passage in the past, I always focused on the behavior of Adam and Eve hiding from God. But this time, a picture formed in my mind of the LORD God walking with his children in the garden in the cool of the day. I realized this is what prayer is all about. God made us so we could walk with him in that garden. Sadly, because of sin, we can no longer join him physically. As a result, prayer is our opportunity to "walk" with God. Prayer is the substitute for what we lost when sin entered the world. It may be a powerful substitute, but it is a far cry from what we will eventually experience when we walk with the LORD God once again in the garden in the cool of the day!

In this context, prayer is an intimate contact with God, not a time to display our religious status before man. All too often prayer, especially corporate prayer, is used to deliver a sermon to those present and not to make an intimate connection with God. Jesus's prayers were different. When others listened to them, they knew he was not talking to them, but directly to the Father. I'm not saying we should avoid praying out loud in groups. Jesus did that. The point is, even when you are in a group, you should enter the private area of your soul, shut out your surroundings, and pray to your Father and no one else. Prayer is a time to walk in the garden in the cool of the day, one-on-one with God. If there are others present, they are only silent observers of an immensely private moment.

PRINCIPLE 3: YOUR SPECIFIC WORDS ARE NOT AS IMPORTANT
AS YOUR HEART

Oftentimes when we pray, we struggle for just the right words. Prayer is treated almost as if it were an incantation. If I could only speak the right set of words to God, then my prayer would be answered, my problem would be solved. It is as if God were the door to Aladdin's cave. The door remains shut until the right sentence is spoken. Like Aladdin, we struggle in our prayers to find our own version of "open sesame."

God is not interested in the specific words we select to express ourselves. Consider this—during his three-year ministry, Jesus constantly prayed, yet few of his prayers are recorded. I suspect that is because if they were, all we would do is repeat them over and over again. We would treat the prayers of Jesus as our open sesame, expecting the same response God gave Jesus. But God is not interested in hearing us repeat what Jesus said. He wants us to speak from our hearts. He wants us to express how we feel, not how we think we should feel or how Jesus felt or what we think God wants to hear. He may want us to pray like Jesus prayed, but he wants it in our own words.

The most famous prayer of Jesus is not really a prayer at all. Even though it is called the Lord's Prayer, Jesus never actually prayed it. He never actually bowed before God and offered this prayer as his own. He simply told the disciples that it was an example of how to pray. Now we repeat it in church. There is nothing wrong with that, but when we do so, we are rarely praying. There is no power in the words of Jesus unless they have become our words as well.

Jesus knew his words could become a substitute for real prayer rather than an example of prayer, so he warned his disciples before he gave them an example. The warning is found in Matthew 6:7–8: "And when you pray, do not keep on babbling like pagans, for they think they will be heard because of their many words. Do not be like them, for your Father knows what you need before you ask him." A better translation of the Greek for "don't babble" is "do not use vain repetitions." In other words, do not repeat prayers or phrases in a vain attempt to make you look good to others, or to God, for that matter.

The reason our words are not as important as our hearts is interesting. Jesus teaches us that the Father already knows what we need before we ask. No amount of flowery words or recitations of the prayers of others will change this simple fact. He doesn't need us to inform him of our needs. He wants us to open our hearts to him through prayer. For example, when Jesus uses the phrase "give us this day our daily bread," it is not so much a request as a reminder and an acknowledgment that God is the source of our daily bread.

Prayer doesn't change God, it changes us. It brings us closer to God. It is our time to walk with him in the garden. It is our opportunity to enter into an intimate relationship with him.

Jesus's prayer in the garden on that dark night before he was arrested was not a plea for God to change, it was a cry for help. He fell on his face before God and asked, "If it is possible, may this cup be taken from me. Yet not as I will, but as you will" (Matthew 26:39). What he asked for that night is less important than what he revealed about his heart. He prayed this simple prayer three times, and each time he exposed both his fear of what was to come and his commitment to obey God.

The Father did not change the path Jesus had to take. Instead, Luke's account tells us he sent an angel to strengthen Jesus in his commitment to the will of the Father. By the end of the third prayer, Jesus was ready to face his destiny. His circumstances were no different than they had been before his prayer, but he was stronger for the encounter.

He went to the disciples and announced, "Look, the hour is near, and the Son of Man is betrayed into the hands of sinners. Rise, let us go! Here comes my betrayer!" (Mark 14:41–42). Jesus was no longer sweating blood. He was ready and determined to face his death. His prayer changed his heart and prepared him to move forward.

PRINCIPLE 4: DON'T ASK GOD TO DO SOMETHING YOU ARE NOT WILLING TO DO YOURSELF

It is important to note there was one thing and only one thing in the Lord's Prayer which Jesus felt the need to explain. Jesus did not comment on the meaning of "your will be done" or the significance of "deliver us from evil." But the phrase "forgive us our debts, as we also have forgiven our debtors" is different. Apparently, it is so important for us to understand what that phrase means in the context of prayer that he did not want his disciples, or us, to miss it.

So Jesus explained, "For if you forgive men when they sin against you, your heavenly Father will also forgive you. But if you do not forgive men their sins, your Father will not forgive your sins" (Matthew 6:15). In essence, Jesus said, "Don't ask God to forgive you if you are unwilling to forgive others."

While this serves as a strong statement of our need to forgive others, remember, Jesus is not trying to teach the apostles about forgiveness here. Rather, his focus is on prayer. In the context of prayer, this lesson takes on a more general meaning.

The broader lesson here is this: don't ask God to do something unless you are willing to participate in the process yourself. For example, don't pray asking God to help the poor if you are able but unwilling to give your time and money to help the poor yourself. Don't ask God to bring a friend to salvation if you are unwilling to share Jesus with that friend. Don't ask God to send you someone to disciple unless you are willing to find someone to disciple. Don't ask God to change your attitude if you are unwilling to change it yourself. Prayer is never a substitute for action; it is a precursor to action. If you want forgiveness, then be forgiving. God wants us to partner with him, not give him orders. God does not want to be told what to do as much as he wants to hear our concerns and what we are willing to do about them in partnership with him.

I believe this principle has a lot to do with what it means to pray in the name of Jesus. The promise we have been given in John 14:13–14 is, "I will do whatever you ask in my name, so that the Son may bring glory to the Father. You may ask me for anything in my name, and I will do it." We tend to believe this means that all we have to do is end our prayer with "in the name of Jesus" and it will be answered. If Jesus was telling the truth, then anything and everything we ask for will be granted if we simply say, "I am asking for this in the name of Jesus." It's as if these are magic words, a doorway into satisfying our every want, another version of open sesame.

But we know it rarely happens that way. The word used in this passage for "name" implies the character and authority of Jesus, not simply invoking his name. Since Jesus never asked God to do something he was not willing to do himself, asking in the name of Jesus means we are not just asking for something from God. We are committing to do something for the kingdom. Asking in the name of Jesus really means we are assuming his authority *as we partner with God* to make something happen. It involves us as much as it involves God.

WHAT SHOULD YOU DO?

Listening to God is an essential part of prayer. You may doubt that God actually talks to you. I did. The church I regularly attended at the time certainly did. But that all changed for me when I attended a class at New Song Church, which was quickly becoming my home church. It's called the Freedom Class, and it is intended to, among other things, introduce us to the God who has always been talking to us. Midway through the five-day course, the teacher, Chris, asked for a volunteer to come up front.

As one brave soul walked forward, Chris told us, "Okay, I want each one of you to pray and ask God to speak to you about Bob. Ask God to tell you something encouraging and then share it with him."

I had never really heard God speak, but I closed my eyes and asked, *God, can you give me something to share with Bob?* Nothing happened. I didn't hear anything; no thoughts popped into my mind; it was all a blank. I was beginning to panic. I pleaded, *God, speak to me, please.*

After a few moments of nothing, Chris spoke up. "Raise your hand if you heard something from God." I looked around, and my worst fear was realized: almost everyone raised their hands. I felt like a failure. One by one, students in the class shared what God had told them about Bob. I began to think that maybe I couldn't hear God, or worse, maybe I was the one person God didn't want to talk to. I hoped neither was true.

In the end, I decided that I would not let one failure separate me from God. I vowed to keep trying. I decided that every prayer time would include some time for God to speak.

It worked. I eventually started to hear God speak. It happened one night when I was praying for a group of InterVarsity student leaders. My goal was to ask God to speak encouraging words to each leader. I was nervous after the experience in the class, but Bonnie was with me, and she definitely heard from God, so if I didn't hear anything, I figured I could rely on what God spoke to her. Then something amazing happened. As I prayed for Sally, one of the students, I saw a picture of her sitting at a table in her apartment, deep in thought as she assembled puzzle pieces. The picture came with a spiritual interpretation meant for her. As I described the picture to her, her roommate started laughing.

"How do you know that?" she said.

I explained, "I don't know, it just came to me. It was like I was sitting across from Sally, watching her. She seemed so focused on the puzzle and so pleased at her progress."

The roommate chuckled again as she told me, "Sally is a biology major, and she has a table in her bedroom with all these DNA puzzle pieces on it. Some nights she will sit for hours putting them together to form some large molecule. When she's done she will come running out to show me the model and tell me how important it is. I usually have no idea what she is talking about."

I was elated. Unless God had shown me, there was no way I could have known that about her. In that moment, God not only gave me encouraging words to speak into her life, he also revealed himself to me.

This has happened to me many times since then. I now understand that God had been speaking to me for a long time, but I only recognized his voice when I relaxed and listened.

None of this means that God doesn't want to hear from us. He certainly does. But what should we ask for? The answer is anything. Just as God invited Solomon to "Ask for whatever you want me to give you" (2 Chronicles 1:7), he welcomes us to share our desires with him. We can learn something from Solomon's response. God is most interested in requests that go to the heart of who we are rather than shortcuts to satisfy a want. Instead of asking God for a new job, ask to be a better worker. Instead of asking for a new car, ask to be a better servant to those in need of transportation. Instead of asking God for more money, ask to be a better steward of what you have. Instead of asking for a friend, ask to be a better friend to others.

Jesus didn't give us a formula for prayer. He didn't give us specific words that must be included. He didn't write down the mechanics of prayer. Instead, he gave us a model prayer life. If I were to summarize that model, it would be this:

- It's not what you say; it's what you hear.
- It's not how long or when you should pray; it's that you should never stop.
- It's not how loud and forceful you are; it's how humble you are.
- It's not what other people hear when you pray; it's what God hears.
- It's not about changing your circumstances; it's about changing your heart.
- It's not about you at all; it's about what the Father is doing.
- It's not about what is on your mind; it's about what is in your heart.

None of these aspects of Jesus's model of prayer should be phrased as a rule. I don't want to recommend a series of specific instructions on how to pray like Jesus, because that would bring us back to the same old trap—just a new set of rules replacing the old ones. However, two points here are important. The first is, always remember that prayer is your time to talk with God as one friend to another. The second is, why would you ever want to say amen? Amen is like hanging up the phone, walking away from your friend, turning off your e-mail, closing the door, driving away. Why would you ever want to say good-bye to God, even for a short period?

Prayer should be like two lovers on the phone where neither can hang up, so for twenty minutes they go back and forth with, "Okay, you hang up first."

"No, you hang up first."

"No, you hang up first."

I am at the point where I never want to hang up.

Chapter Three

LOVE LIKE JESUS LOVED

I don't think I really understood what love was until I had an encounter with a homeless man on the streets of Tacoma. It occurred on my first Sunday morning at the Redemption Outreach Center, the ROC, a church I now co-pastor for the homeless of Tacoma. The ROC opens its doors at 7 a.m., and the service begins at 7:30. The ROC ministry team meets for prayer at 6:30 a.m. and then goes out onto the streets to invite street people up for the service.

I arrived on my first morning just a little frightened, wondering what I had gotten myself into. The homeless had always been scary to me. They were dirty, smelly, and most likely mentally ill or on drugs. Yet somehow God had prompted me to volunteer to help out. I thought I would just be an usher or hand out hot chocolate to the people as they came, but instead, the team leader told me to go out and invite people in. This was way beyond my comfort zone, since I am by nature shy.

As soon as I stepped out the door, I saw a large, burly African-American leaning up against the church. I walked up to him, sucked in my breath, offered my hand, and said, "Hi, my name is Rick." I hoped he didn't see my knees shaking. This was one big, scary dude.

"Rufus," he said.

I have never been good at small talk, so my mind raced. "Well, how are you doing, Rufus?"

There was a pause. As we stared at each other I recognized a sadness in him, and to my surprise, my initial fear melted away. Rufus must have noticed it, because he visibly changed.

"Things aren't going well for me at all," he replied.

"What's going on? What happened?" I asked him.

Rufus explained, "Last night at the shelter, someone stole everything

I had while I was sleeping. I lost my ID, my clothes, everything. I don't know what I'm going to do now."

Any residue of fear was totally gone. My heart broke for him. "Rufus, I am so sorry. Can I pray for you?" I asked.

"Yes."

I placed my hand on his shoulder and asked God to protect his precious child. As I prayed, this big man started to cry. In that brief moment, I showed Rufus something he had not experienced for a long time, and I found something inside of me that I did not know could be so easily tapped. It's called love. The warmth of a human touch, the concern of a stranger, the realization that God loved him—all this reminded Rufus of his worth.

Rufus and I became great friends. I looked forward to talking with him every Sunday. After several years, he disappeared. I often wonder what happened to him. I pray he found a place to call his own. I will always remember how a simple gesture on a cold rainy morning had the power to restore dignity and teach me something about the power of love.

Love is a powerful force in the universe. Love is the great motivator in art, literature, film, and life. Love inspires us to be better people, to be creative, to seek the company of others. Love is the glue that binds relationships. There would be no relationships without love and no expression of love without relationships. Much as the earth was at the beginning, life would be formless, empty, and dark without love.

Nothing characterizes the life of Jesus more than the single word *love*. As the Creator, he forged us in the fire of love. As the Savior, he sacrificed himself out of love. As our Friend, he pursues us because of his love. If we are to do what Jesus did, then we must love as Jesus loved.

The central, foundational importance of love should come as no surprise. God's love was the force behind the creation of Adam. Our inherent need to love others is the reason he created Eve. Up until then, God had pronounced everything he made as good. But when he saw Adam standing alone in the midst of his marvelous creation, he knew something was not right. Adam was missing something important, someone to love, someone to join him. He wasn't complete. Adam had a relationship with God, but God recognized that even a relationship with him was not enough for Adam. It may seem surprising, and even somewhat shocking, to say that. If anyone other than God had said this, we would reject it out of hand! But from the beginning, we were created to love. Jefferson Airplane captured it so well when they wrote the song, "Don't You Want Somebody to Love."

Created in the image of God, we all need someone to love. As a result, it is no surprise that the enemy has done everything he can to undermine our innate drive to love others and to pervert our understanding of love. Jesus had to come to earth to teach us, once again, how to love.

WHAT IS LOVE?

Jesus said, "A new command I give you: Love one another. *As I have loved you, so you must love one another.* By this all men will know that you are my disciples, if you love one another" (John 12:34–35). This command is not just to love, but to love like Jesus loved. This is fundamentally different from what the world considers to be love. It is so distinctive it should make believers stand out from the rest of the world. It is so powerful that we will witness to the world not by the words we say, but by the love we display.

Paul emphasized this point in Galatians 5:6: "For in Christ Jesus neither circumcision nor uncircumcision has any value. The only thing that counts is faith expressing itself through love." Faith, which is the same thing as belief, which is the same thing as trusting God, is manifested through the kind of love Jesus modeled.

But what exactly is love? The formal definition is "an emotion of strong affection," but those words hardly seem to capture the true nature of love. Love is far more than can be expressed by mere words. It is a mother's soft caress of her baby. It is the sparkle in the eye of a proud father. It is the joy in the hearts of a couple on their wedding day. It is the sacrifice one friend makes for another.

Paul provided a beautiful definition of love in 1 Corinthians 13. He wrote that love is patient and kind, as well as protective, trusting, and hopeful—but even his definition is more in terms of what love is not. He wrote that love does not envy, does not boast, is not proud, rude, evil, angry, or self-seeking. Love is hard to capture in a word, a phrase, a sentence, or a paragraph.

Whatever love is, one thing is clear: love is a powerful force. As an indication of its power, Jesus gave what on the surface would appear to be an unexpected response when a Pharisee, an expert in the law, asked him, "What is the greatest commandment?" (Matthew 22:36). I would have expected Jesus to say all ten commandments were important. How could he pick just one, in effect saying that if you are only going to obey one, this is it? Aren't we supposed to obey them all? Yet, he answered the Pharisee's question by saying,

> "Love the Lord your God with all your heart and with all your soul and with all your mind." This is the first and greatest commandment. And the second is like it: "Love your neighbor as yourself." All the Law and the Prophets hang on these two commandments. (Matthew 22:37–40)

The Pharisee wanted to know which commandment was greatest, and Jesus gave him two commandments to obey. They both deal with the issue of love. While love covers a multitude of sins (1 Peter 4:8), it is even more powerful than that—it is at the foundation of all the law and all the prophets. Every command of God and every statement made by the prophets in the name of the Lord can be summarized in one phrase: love God and your neighbor. If you obey the first, then you can't help but obey the second. If you disobey the second, there is no way you can obey the first. If you obey them both, you automatically fulfill the law.

Paul characterized love in terms of the best of human nature without the worst of human behavior. Jesus described love as the power behind the law. While both reveal the enduring nature of love, they still do not answer the broader question—what is love?

Perhaps the answer can be found at the beginning of time. When God created Eve, he called her a helper. The word used in Genesis for "helper" is derived from the Hebrew word *azar*, meaning "to surround," and it carries the implication of protecting and aiding. It is used in Daniel 10:12 to mean "stand beside to deliver" and in Ezra 10:15 to mean "support." In this light, love is a total surrender of self-interest, a commitment to surround, protect, and help another, putting the other's needs above your own. In some small way, that is what I found myself doing for Rufus on that cold Sunday morning. As I listened to him, touched him, and prayed for him, I was for a brief moment his helper, supporting him though his difficult time.

The traditional wedding vows speak of "forsaking all others." Perhaps a better way to capture the nature of a loving marriage commitment would be to vow to "forsake myself." We need people in our lives who will make that commitment to us, and we need to make that commitment to others. It is how we were designed by God.

WHY IS LOVE SO DIFFICULT?

Love should be easy. We need it. We want to give it. We were designed to love each other. What happened to make it so hard to love?

Love is difficult for two reasons: sin inserted itself into love, and the world corrupted the idea of love. The first consequence of sin was exactly what God told Adam and Eve it would be: death entered the world. The second consequence was the distortion of love. This happened when God asked Adam, "Have you eaten from the tree that I commanded you not to eat from?" (Genesis 3:11). Adam should have answered honestly with a simple "yes." Instead, he said something that forever changed our concept of love. He told God, "The woman you put here with me—she gave me some fruit from the tree, and I ate it" (Genesis 3:12). In a pathetic attempt to minimize his own guilt, Adam tried to pass as much blame as possible on to Eve.

Imagine Eve, standing beside Adam, listening to those words. The man whom she trusted, who was supposed to surround her, protect her, and put her needs before his own, had sold her out. While Adam did not have a responsibility to hide Eve's sin, he did have a responsibility to fully accept his own guilt without bringing Eve into it. Unfortunately,

Adam chose to violate Eve's trust and thereby change the reality of love as mankind knew it. From that moment on, Eve could not longer completely trust Adam. Adam, discovering the untrustworthiness within himself, feared the worst in Eve. Both understood they had to keep a part of themselves secret or risk rejection. Thus, the seeds of jealousy and control were planted into all future relationships. So much went wrong that day—so much of what love really is was lost.

The enemy continues to do everything possible to confuse our understanding of love. Rather than teaching that love is a selfless commitment, the world teaches that love is something that just happens to us. Love is a force beyond our control. We fall into it and just as easily fall out of it. Love has become confused with lust.

The world also confuses love with ownership. What we love belongs to us. With ownership comes control. Rather than stand by and protect those we love, we dominate and possess them. This has led some to stalk, terrorize, and even murder those they profess to love. All this confusion over the true nature of love leads us to do horrible, decidedly unloving things.

The beautiful passage Paul wrote about love in 1 Corinthians 13 has been turned upside down by the world. If someone were to describe love in the world's terms today, their attempt might read, "Love is frustrating, love is bitter. It is possessive, it bullies, it is self-seeking, it is intolerant, it keeps long records of hurts. Love does not delight in sacrifice but rejoices in retribution. It is always self-protecting, rarely trusting, easily discouraged, always ready to give up."

No wonder so many young people today struggle with the concept of love! They don't have any good examples to teach them what love really is—except for one.

How Did Jesus Love?

Knowing the world would pollute the concept of love, Jesus came to show us how to love. He didn't wait long before he gave us the initial lesson. The first action of Jesus after he was anointed at his baptism is saturated with the power of love.

Jesus's lessons on love began with the third temptation recorded in Matthew 4:8–11.

> Again, the devil took him to a high mountain and showed him all the kingdoms of the world and their splendor. "All this I will give you," he said, "if you will bow down and worship me." Jesus said to him, "Away from me, Satan! For it is written: 'Worship the Lord your God, and serve him only.'" Then the devil left him, and angels came and attended him.

This is the final temptation the enemy placed before Jesus. After the first two failed, Satan brought out the big guns and offered Jesus what he believed Jesus wanted most: the return of his control over all the earth. Satan never really wanted to rule us; he wanted to be above God, so he was willing to return us to God if Jesus would worship him. Satan's fatal flaw was that he did not understand the power of love. He believed that all Jesus had come to do was reclaim his authority over us, to win back what he had lost. In effect, Satan said to Jesus, "You don't have to die to buy these people back. I will give them to you so you can rule over them. All you have to do is acknowledge my preeminence." Satan saw this last temptation as a win-win situation. They both would get what they wanted. Jesus to rule, Satan to dominate.

The temptation failed on so many levels! Jesus would never bow to the enemy because he served the Father. Besides, Satan did not offer Jesus what he had really come to acquire. Jesus did not come to rule over us. Jesus was not seeking power or control. He was seeking a relationship. He didn't come to win back what he lost in the garden; he came to restore to us what we lost. Jesus wanted to be our friend, not our master. Jesus loved us so much he turned away from the easy path in favor of the only one that would lead to our redemption. No matter what it cost, Jesus would not compromise his goal. Jesus would die to purchase our friendship rather than save himself just to reign over us.

This is his first lesson on love, and it clearly illustrates the Genesis concept of love as something that surrounds and protects. Jesus stood between us and Satan that day on the mountaintop, protecting us from the ultimate consequence of our sin.

Jesus later explained exactly what had happened during that third temptation in John 15:12–16:

> My command is this: Love each other as I have loved you. Greater love has no one than this, that he lay down his life for his friends. You are my friends if you do what I command. I no longer call you servants, because a servant does not know his master's business. Instead, I have called you friends, for everything that I learned from my Father I have made known to you.

Jesus demonstrated the greatest love of all: he was willing to lay down his life not for his subjects, for his servants, or even for what rightly belonged to him. On that mountaintop, when Satan thought he had made an offer Jesus couldn't refuse, Jesus did something Satan did not expect. He committed himself to die for his friends.

I can only imagine the frustration Satan experienced at that moment. As he slunk away, he must have thought, *What is wrong with Jesus? Mankind disobeys God, does horrible things to each other, and they are going to reject and kill him. Why does he willingly submit to all of that?*

Yet it was precisely in that moment that Jesus taught us what love really is. As Paul was to write later, "Love…endures all things" (1 Corinthians 13:7, NKJV). Love, as Jesus lived it, endures everything—not some things, not just the unintentional slight or the occasional wrong, but even death. The enemy does not understand this kind of love, and that is why he will lose.

Three years later, Jesus died on the cross, remaining firm to the commitment he made when he turned down Satan's offer at the beginning of his ministry. During those years between the temptation and his death, he had lived a life filled with love. He had endured hypocrisy, betrayal, rejection, ridicule, slander, and hatred, yet he never once wavered from his love for those who turned on him. In the midst of his excruciating pain while hanging on that cross, he continued to teach us what love really is as he cried out, "Father, forgive them."

What a contrast to the actions of Adam! Rather than turn on us as Adam turned on Eve, Jesus continued to surround us with his love. He remained our protector. He came to our aid, ignoring the cost. That one act reverberates throughout eternity with the words, "I love you more than life itself." Where Adam failed, Jesus succeeded, restoring the true meaning of love.

This is how Jesus loved. This is what he came to teach us about love. This is what we are commanded to imitate. Jesus loved without condition, without expectation, without boundaries. He taught us that love is not a reward; it is a gift. It is not earned; it is dispensed. It is not restrained; it is released.

How Then Should We Love?

Loving like Jesus loved begins when we restore what Adam lost. Loving like Jesus loved means becoming the helper we were designed to be. All the things that define the biblical term "helper" are embodied in Paul's 1 Corinthians 13 definition of love, which "always protects [and] always trusts."

Here is the hard part. Jesus taught something else about love that is totally different from the world's concept of love. In the world's view, love, to be healthy and viable, must be returned. Love must be mutual and balanced, or it is doomed to fail. Jesus taught a completely different form of love. He said in Luke 6:32–34,

> If you love those who love you, what credit is that to you? Even "sinners" love those who love them. And if you do good to those who are good to you, what credit is that to you? Even "sinners" do that. And if you lend to those from whom you expect repayment, what credit is that to you? Even "sinners" lend to "sinners," expecting to be repaid in full.

The world not only teaches that love must be returned, it advocates revenge against those who harm us, rejection of those who mistreat us, and hatred toward those who hate us. We are to love only those who are lovable.

Jesus, on the other hand, didn't die for those who loved him. He died for people who mocked him while he hung on the cross. He died for the Pharisees who hated him and brought him to trial. He died for us, not after we professed love for him, but "while we were still sinners" (Romans 5:8).

Jesus taught this new kind of love several times during his ministry. When he taught it in Matthew 5:43–45, it caught the attention of his Jewish audience: "You have heard that it was said, 'Love your neighbor and hate your enemy.' But I tell you: Love your enemies and pray for those who persecute you, that you may be sons of your Father in heaven."

To the Jews of his time, "love your enemies" clearly meant something different from what they thought God intended, because Jesus started with a strange comment: "You have heard that it was said, 'Love your neighbor and hate your enemy.'" Evidently, religious Jews were taught to hate their enemies. But when did God say that?

This teaching was apparently based on Leviticus 19:17–18: "Do not hate your brother in your heart. Rebuke your neighbor frankly so you will not share in his guilt. Do not seek revenge or bear a grudge against one of *your people,* but love your neighbor as yourself." Accordingly, the Jews used the phrase "your people" as the definition of "your neighbor." Loving their neighbor only required them to love other Jews. They were free to hate their Gentile enemies.

Imagine their surprise to learn they had missed the heart of the message in Leviticus 19 when Jesus told them they should love their enemies. Jesus made this clear when he was directly asked, "Okay, then, who is our neighbor?" (Luke 10:29). He answered the question with the story of the Good Samaritan. In essence, Jesus told them that their hated enemies, the Samaritans, not only understood the meaning of neighbor better than they did, but that the Samaritans *were* their neighbor.

This teaching was not just an academic exercise for Jesus. It characterized his life. Jesus had more enemies than friends. His enemies hated him for what he represented. They beat him at his trial. They stole from him, cursed him, and finally killed him. Yet he loved them. Jesus responded to his enemies in just the way he told others to in Luke 6:27–31, 35:

> But I tell you who hear me: Love your enemies, do good to those who hate you, bless those who curse you, pray for those who mistreat you. If someone strikes you on one cheek, turn to him the other also. If someone takes your cloak, do not stop him from taking your tunic. Give to everyone who asks you, and if anyone takes what belongs to you, do not demand it back. Do to others as you would have them do to you. But love your enemies, do good to them, and lend to them without expecting to get anything back.

Like Jesus, our enemies are those who hate us, strike us, steal from us, or curse us. If we are to do what Jesus did, then we are to love them. This is how Paul lived, as he described his life in 1 Corinthians 4:12–13: "When we are cursed, we bless; when we are persecuted, we endure it; when we are slandered, we answer kindly."

Loving our enemies involves far more than expressing a positive emotion toward them. It requires us to take action on their behalf. We are told to pray for them, bless them, give to them, and do good to them. We are to do all this without any expectation that they will suddenly turn from their hatred. It is the stuff of Hollywood that the "bad guy" responds to love with a total transformation by the end of the movie, but it rarely happens in real life. As imitators of Jesus, we are not to expect a dramatic repentance from those who hurt us. Remember, "Love endures all things," and that includes a continuous negative response.

Regardless of the response or lack of response of our enemy to our love, we can take hope in one thing. Paul tells us in 1 Corinthians 13:8 that "Love never fails." If love never fails, then hate, and even indifference, *never* succeed. This is especially true of religious hate.

There is a pastor traveling around the US today invading the funerals of fallen soldiers. He and members of his church carry painful, hateful signs supposedly in the name of Jesus. The signs say "Thank God for dead soldiers" and proclaim that "God hates the US." Whatever his goal might be, it is doomed to failure. His work is certainly not what Jesus would do. This pastor's actions do not single him out as a disciple of Jesus Christ. No matter how strongly he feels that members of the military or US government are his enemies, his public displays of hate will never succeed. If only he would take the words of Jesus to heart and shower love on his perceived enemies, he might find that Jesus has a lesson to teach him.

Loving others as Jesus loves them is difficult because it calls for a radical restoration of the true nature of love in our lives. It requires us not only to love, but to become trustworthy. It asks us to make a commitment to others that goes beyond the world's standards. God understands that this is hard because it requires us to tear down interpersonal barriers built up over a lifetime. But even if it can't be done all at once, it can be done one step at a time.

Begin by asking the Holy Spirit to allow you to see those around you as Jesus sees them. Ask him to show you their potential, not their failings. React to the latent possibilities within them and not to the external manifestations of a hurt soul. Respond to their needs, not their demands. I have discovered, as I work with people on the streets in some of the poorest areas of the world, that love does not require giving money, food, or clothing. Those things may be helpful, but sometimes love, as Jesus expressed it, comes in the form of a simple gesture of understanding, a brief affirmation of the worth of another human being, just as I discovered that morning I first met Rufus.

I have learned that loving as Jesus loved is not as hard as it once sounded. It is enough to do what Heidi Baker, the founder of Iris Ministries, recommends: "Love the one in front of you." You can surely do that.

Chapter Four

SERVE LIKE JESUS SERVED

I teach computer science at Pacific Lutheran University. One day, I was not feeling well at work. Being diabetic, I immediately recognized the feeling as low blood sugar. I needed to get something to eat, so I drove off campus to a fast-food place. While I was driving back, I passed three women standing by the side of the road. I thought they were just waiting for a ride, but the Lord told me I should stop to help them. I didn't know what to say—so I drove on.

Two blocks down the road, I decided I needed to obey God even though I had no clue about what I could do. I turned around and pulled up in front of the women. Still not knowing what to say, I got out of the car and walked up to one of them. "I don't really know what I am doing," I said, "but God sent me. He said I could help you. Can I?" The words that came out of my mouth surprised me as much as the three women.

One of them started to cry. "I was just thrown out of my apartment. Everything I own is up there." She pointed to a tarp under a tree just up the road. "I have a storage area rented, but no way to move these boxes. Would you be willing to put them in your van?"

I had an old Dodge minivan, the kind with a backseat that could roll out to make room for extra storage. I took the seat out and put it by the side of the road. I figured that if I was doing God's work, he would look after it! We loaded her goods into the van and took them to her storage area. It took two loads to move everything. When we were done, I found my backseat undisturbed, sitting where I had left it. I put it back in my car and returned to my office.

I had not wanted to stop to help this woman. I thought I had nothing to offer. In fact, I thought I would just sound silly and appear foolish. I was scared, but I obeyed anyway, and God blessed me in ways I had never experienced before. I was slowly learning that to unleash the power of God in my life, I needed to give up control and be willing to serve others even when it made me uncomfortable.

When I got back to my office, I stopped to think about the last words she had said to me: "You are a godsend." My first response was no, all I did was stop to help. Then I realized that she was right. That day, because I obeyed God, I was in every literal sense of the word a God-send. That day was my first lesson in serving like Jesus served.

Because Jesus loved us, he came to serve, not to rule over us. In the process, he taught us a lesson about both love and service. They are inseparable. To love means to serve, and service is an expression of love. Just like faith without works is dead, love without service is meaningless. You may profess love for someone, but if you are not willing to put their needs ahead of your own, it is a hollow, empty profession.

In fact, the connection between love and service is so strong that I believe the two most important commandments could be rewritten without changing their meaning. Instead of "Love the Lord your God with all your heart and with all your soul and with all your mind...and the second is like it: Love your neighbor as yourself," it would make just as much sense to say, "*Serve* the Lord your God with all your heart and with all your soul and with all your mind...and the second is like it: *serve* your neighbor as yourself." I am not in the habit of rewriting Scripture, but in this case it makes sense when service is defined as God defines it. Paul said as much in his letter to the Galatians: "Do not use your freedom to indulge the sinful nature; rather, serve one another in love. The entire law is summed up in a single command: 'Love your neighbor as yourself'" (Galatians 5:13–14). Paul understood that "serving one another in love" is the same thing as "loving your neighbor as yourself."

Given this tight connection between love and service, it follows that to love like Jesus loved means to serve like Jesus served. But how are we to do this? How did Jesus serve others, and how can we imitate him?

WHAT IS SERVICE?

Christians do not hold a monopoly on important works of service. For every Mother Teresa, there is a Mahatma Gandhi. Believers and nonbelievers do not part ways over the meaning of service, but rather over the motivation for service. Nonbelievers serve others out of compassion, a sense of mission, and a desire to give back to the community. These are good and noble reasons. They motivate believers as well.

But Christians serve for another reason. They serve because they are working for Jesus. Actually, it goes even deeper than that. One day, while teaching the disciples, Jesus told them that the King would bless the righteous because they fed him when he was hungry, clothed him when he was cold, and helped him when he was sick. Surprised, the righteous will ask, "Lord, when did we see you hungry and feed you, or thirsty and give you something to drink? When did we see you a stranger and invite you in, or needing clothes and clothe you? When did we see you sick or in prison and go to visit you?" And the King would reply, "I tell you the truth, whatever you did for one of the least of these brothers of mine, you did for me" (Matthew 25:37–40). Christians serve others not just because they are doing it *for* the Lord, but because they are doing it *to* the Lord. This is the kind of service that is motivated by love.

It may seem like splitting hairs to draw a distinction between Christian service and non-Christian service based solely on the role Jesus plays in Christian work. Both Christian and non-Christian organizations make valuable contributions to society. Yet, there is a subtle and significant difference between service motivated solely by compassion and service motivated both by compassion and love for the Lord. While the world may see the needy as projects, believers serve the needy not out of Christian duty but as a glorious opportunity to minister to Jesus himself. The focus on the ones being served becomes not how far they have fallen but how high they can rise.

Christians see the needy not as people trapped by unfortunate circumstances, but as victims of an evil, powerful, cold, and heartless enemy. That enemy has robbed them of far more than their material well-being. He has stolen their potential in Christ. Therefore, the goal of Christian service goes beyond providing food, clothing, or shelter. Christian service seeks to defeat the enemy who brought so much ruin into their lives in the first place.

In a word, *Christian service is war.* A war fought one person, one family, one community at a time. It is a war against injustice in which Christian service has a distinct advantage over secular service. By serving God while serving others, we have access to the power of God. As a result, we have a higher level of expectation when we serve. We expect to see the impossible happen. We expect the addict to be released from addiction. We expect the sick to be healed. We expect the hungry to be fed. And we expect all of this regardless of the circumstances. When Christians serve in the name of Christ, there is always enough to meet the need.

How Did Jesus Serve?

Throughout his life, Jesus performed many acts of service. He healed the sick, forgave the guilty, fed the hungry, taught the needy, gave rest to the tired, and ultimately laid down his life for us. His very first miracle, changing water into wine at a wedding, was an act of pure service. Each act was a living illustration of love.

We are called to imitate Jesus's service, but what does that mean? Are we to help everyone who asks for it? Should we give money to causes? Should we invest our time and energy working with the needy? Should we pray for those who need it? Is one type of service better than another? The list of questions goes on and on because the concept of service has so many different dimensions.

Rather than looking at specific actions, then, it is more valuable to explore some general principles of service. We can use these principles as a guide to serving like Jesus served. I believe that serving like Jesus served comes down to four principles common to every act of service he performed:

- Service always begins by serving God.
- Service always comes at a price.
- Service is never done for the sake of a material reward.
- Service always glorifies God.

PRINCIPLE ONE: SERVICE ALWAYS BEGINS BY SERVING GOD

If the difference between the nature of our service and that of nonbelievers lies in our ultimate motivation, what is that motivation? It is not, as some might suspect, a motivation to bring those we serve to Christ. We would love to see that happen, but we don't serve others for that reason alone, and in fact, we are not told to do so in the Word. Rather, we serve others out of pure love. A love that originates from our love for God and our desire to serve him.

From the beginning, God made it clear that we were to serve him and him alone. Deuteronomy 6:13 says, "Fear the LORD your God, serve him only." Joshua told his people, "Now fear the LORD and serve him with all faithfulness" (Joshua 24:14). Paul broadened the concept of service in his letter to the church at Ephesus: "Serve wholeheartedly, as if you were serving the Lord, not men" (Ephesians 6:70). We are called to serve God, but for us, serving others is the same thing as serving God.

Because we first serve God, our service to others takes on a new dimension. We are able to move into the realm of the supernatural. Our goal is not to just provide relief from immediate physical deprivation; it is to bring the wealth of heaven to earth. Our goal is not just to save the poor and needy from their circumstances, it is to deliver them from their captivity. Our goal is not to just satisfy their needs, it is to bring them a peace that "transcends all understanding" (Philippians 4:7). Our goal cannot be achieved in the natural. It requires the supernatural. And we can tap into that resource because we serve God first.

One of the first times I saw this difference remains as a milestone in my understanding of godly service. I led a group to a remote village in the mountains of the Philippines. We distributed food, medicine, and nursing care, just as any other humanitarian relief organization would do. But we also brought something else with us—something that went beyond the normal boundaries of traditional service. We brought the One we serve first—God. This made a tremendous difference in what we could do. We not only distributed goods, we sat with people and prayed with them. We addressed both their physical and emotional scars with supernatural power. As a result, people were healed in ways that traditional medicine and a few days' worth of food could never have accomplished.

The day we arrived in the village, several of us prayed for people at the front of the partially constructed church we used as our base in the village. About midday, an old man slowly shuffled in. He sat down in front of us. Through an interpreter, he explained, "I have arthritis in my ankles and hips. I can barely walk. I am in constant pain, but I know God can heal me. Will you pray?"

Three of us laid hands on him and prayed that God would heal him. We rebuked the pain, commanded the joints to heal, and asked the Holy Spirit to fill him with comfort.

"Are you feeling any better?" I asked.

"I feel some warmth, and the pain seems to have gone down a little," he replied.

He stood up. As he walked away, it looked to me like he could take longer strides than before, but he was definitely still in pain. He left us with the declaration, "I know that when I wake up in the morning, I will be healed."

He didn't have to wait that long. A half-hour later, he ran (that's right, ran) through the village, his hand pointing to the sky, yelling "Jesus healed me, Jesus healed me!" I was excited, both because he was restored and because he knew where the credit belonged. A year later I went back to the same village and found him still walking and still praising God. As servants of God, doing his work in his power, just as Jesus taught us, we can achieve so much more.

Principle Two: Service Always Comes at a Price

Unfortunately, service is often what we do with what we have left over. I speak from experience because, for too many years, that is what I did. To some, service means giving things to the poor that would ordinarily be thrown away. It is giving extra funds left over at the end of the month to some organization. It is spending spare time, when it can be found, working with the needy.

All of these things are good and needed, but they are not the kind of service Jesus performed. Jesus did not give from his abundance, he gave from his core. He gave up everything: his status as God, his rights as the Creator, even his life.

He told us what he expects in Luke 12:48: "From everyone who has been given much, much will be demanded; and from the one who has been entrusted with much, much more will be asked."

The message is clear. If "much" is the measure of what we are given, then "much" is what we are to give away. If we have been entrusted with much, then we are to give "much more." The command is not, "To whom much has been given, if any extra is found, then give it away." What we have is what we are to give. Service cannot be separated from sacrifice.

Every act of service on the part of Jesus involved sacrifice. From his coming as a human to his death on the cross and everything in between, he gave "much more."

Long before Jesus came to teach us about service, David understood both this responsibility and its cost. When God instructed David to build an altar on the threshing floor of Araunah the Jebusite to bring an end to a plague in Israel, David went to the site. He found Araunah and explained that he wanted to buy the land for an altar. Araunah offered to give the land to David, "But King David replied to Araunah, 'No, I insist on buying it for the full price. I will not take what is yours and give it to the Lord. *I will not present burnt offerings that have cost me nothing!*'" (1 Chronicles 21:24).

PRINCIPLE THREE: NEVER SERVE FOR A MATERIAL REWARD

There is always a reward for service, especially when that service follows the model laid down by Jesus. Jesus taught us in Luke 6:38 to "Give, and it will be given to you." Paul wrote in 2 Corinthians 9:6 that "He who sows bountifully shall also reap bountifully." The Bible mentions rewards over and over again.

The real issue is not whether there will be a reward for our service, but whether a material reward is our motivation for service. If you are serving with the expectation of a material reward, then you are not performing a service, you are selling your skills. What should be sacrificial service becomes nothing more than a business transaction. "I will help the poor because I will get even more back in return" is not a motivation that defines service. Jesus addressed this issue when he said, "But when you give to the needy, do not let your left hand know what your right hand is doing, so that your giving may be in secret. Then your Father, who sees what is done in secret, will reward you" (Matthew 6:3–4). Doing something in secret doesn't only mean hiding your service from men. The secret is meant to be kept from ourselves. Jesus was telling us we shouldn't give with our left hand while at the same time holding out our right hand to receive something in return. Instead, we should wait patiently for the spiritual reward God promises us.

God made the people of Israel a promise much like the one Jesus made in Luke 6:

> "Bring the whole tithe into the storehouse, that there may be food in my house. Test me in this," says the LORD Almighty, "and see if I will not throw open the floodgates of heaven and pour out so much blessing that you will not have room enough for it. I will prevent pests from devouring your crops, and the vines in your fields will not cast their fruit," says the LORD Almighty. "Then all the nations will call you blessed, for yours will be a delightful land," says the LORD Almighty. (Malachi 3:10–12)

The reason Israel had not received this promise is revealed in Malachi 3:14–15:

> You have said, "It is futile to serve God. What did we gain by carrying out his requirements and going about like mourners before the LORD Almighty? But now we call the arrogant blessed.

Certainly the evildoers prosper, and even those who challenge
God escape."

In other words, they had only served God because they expected an
immediate material reward, and when it didn't come quickly, they
stopped serving him. Because they could see no immediate gain from
their contributions, because they saw those who didn't serve God prosper, they stopped their service to God. Their expectations were their
downfall.

I can't tell you how many conferences I have attended where the
leaders have asked for donations using Luke 6:38 or 2 Corinthians 9:6
as motivation. God bless them. They were using biblical truth. But I always felt uncomfortable when they did. I didn't want to give because I
expected to get it all back. I wanted to give because I wanted to serve. I
wanted to give because I wanted to help. I wanted to give for the pure
joy of giving. I wanted to give because I wanted to meet the needs of others, not because I wanted more for myself. When I give with my left
hand, I don't want to focus on what I will get back in my right; instead,
I want to focus on the spiritual treasures in heaven, the joy, the peace,
the contentment that are the real rewards for service.

Peter warned us not to give out of desire for more in 1 Peter 5:2: "Be
shepherds of God's flock that is under your care, serving as overseers—
not because you must, but because you are willing, as God wants you to
be; not greedy for money, but eager to serve." We should not appeal to
greed with promises of more material gain in return for service, even if
God has promised to give us more. We should instead appeal to what is,
in the words of Paul, ". . . true, whatever is noble, whatever is right, whatever is pure, whatever is lovely, whatever is admirable" (Philippians 4:8).

Jesus served without thought of what he would gain on earth in return. He had everything. He was God. He was the Creator. He had spent
an eternity with the Father and the Holy Spirit. He gave it all up to become human, to suffer, and to be rejected not only by his creation, but
by the Father at the moment he took on our sins and ultimately died.
He didn't do this because he knew he would get everything back. He

certainly didn't do it for money. He didn't do it because he wanted to rule over us. He did it for one reason: "Jesus...who for the joy set before him endured the cross, scorning its shame" (Hebrews 12:2). He did it for the joy of seeing us in heaven. He did it for the spiritual reward of an eternal relationship with us. Our salvation is his reward, his joy. Herein lies the secret to service as modeled by Jesus. The only real reward is not a material return on your investment; instead, it is a lasting relationship with God.

As the executive director of the Kingdom is Near Ministries, I was invited to speak at a church to describe our mission. As I prayed about my message, God gave me the story of David and Goliath.

At first I wondered what this had to do with serving the poor. Then God gave me a new take on the story. He told me to think about the pebbles David used, and the story took on a whole new level of meaning. Those pebbles in the nearby stream had been stepped on or kicked out of the way as soldiers marched to the battlefield. No one except David saw them for what they really were—powerful weapons that could bring down the enemy. The poor, in whom our ministry had discovered such power and authority, were just like those pebbles. We were like David. We saw their potential and had been called to mobilize them. But the pebbles would have been useless to David if it were not for the sling. The sling empowered the pebbles and sent them to their target.

God told me that in our service, all Christians are like one of these three players. Some are Davids who recognize and mobilize that which others have ignored. Some are pebbles who have been overlooked for so long, yet have immense authority. Some are slings who, through their work and gifts, launch the pebbles. The Goliaths of this world would dominate if we did not work together to bring them down.

None of these worked for a material reward. The Davids of this world do not search out the overlooked because they expect great power. The pebbles do not bring down their targets because they expect praise. And the slings that hurl the pebbles at their target do not do so because they expect great riches on earth. They all serve because they have the same goal: to bring down the ones who blaspheme the Almighty.

PRINCIPLE FOUR: SERVICE ALWAYS GLORIFIES GOD

Given that service comes at a price and that we should never expect a material reward even if through the grace of God one might come, what should be our motivation? Selflessness, certainly. Sacrifice, without a doubt. But good people who do not believe in Jesus could and do perform selfless, sacrificial service. The real motivation for our service should be something different. Just as the love we display should be different from the love the world displays, our service should be different in such a way that we identify ourselves as followers of Jesus.

This was Paul's instruction in 2 Corinthians 9:13: "Remember that men will know we are followers of Jesus by our love and they will also praise God because of our service." We serve others because it glorifies God and leads others to praise God. That is what should set us apart from others who also serve in this world. This is the model Jesus showed us. When he raised Lazarus from the dead, he performed a miraculous service for Mary, Martha, and certainly Lazarus, but that is not how he described it. Instead Jesus said, "This sickness will not end in death. No, it is for God's glory so that God's Son may be glorified through it" (John 11:4). Jesus explained to Philip that whatever he did was to glorify the Father: "And I will do whatever you ask in my name, so that the Son may bring glory to the Father" (John 14:13).

Our service has the same purpose as Jesus's. He told the disciples, "This is to my Father's glory, that you bear much fruit, showing yourselves to be my disciples" (John 15:8).

HOW SHOULD WE SERVE?

All service, Christian and secular, begins with a level of compassion and a sense of mercy for those in need. Christian service adds another dimension, a focus on serving God. When we do that, something amazing happens. The Holy Spirit fills us with gifts that multiply our ability to serve.

The purpose of these gifts is described in 1 Peter 4:10: "Each one should use whatever gift he has received to serve others, faithfully administering God's grace in its various forms." In one short sentence, Peter captures the essence of service. First, everyone should be involved in service. The world is not divided into three groups: those who serve, those who need service, and those who watch others serve. Instead, there is only one group: those who serve others. No one is exclusively a project for someone else. People who receive help also have the capacity to help others. Even when you are in need, there is someone else out there who needs you.

I see this truth lived out every Sunday morning. After the church service at the ROC, our host church offers a breakfast for the homeless. They feed up to two hundred people. It is staffed entirely by volunteers, many of whom are homeless themselves. The homeless help cook the meal, set up, take down the tables, clean the area, and wash the dishes. There are always more volunteers than needed. It is a clear lesson that those who need help can still serve others.

The second truth Peter captured is that all Christians have a gift for service. This is not just an ordinary gift. It is a supernatural gift. The Greek word Peter used here is *charisma,* which means "a miraculous capability." This is a gift that allows you to give more than you think you can give, to do more than is humanly possible, and to see results that defy the imagination.

The third truth actually defines service. It is "faithfully administering God's grace." In the end, we are only the agents of God's grace to the needy. Service is not about us at all. It is not our money that feeds the hungry. It is not our hands that heal the sick. It is not our compassion that brings hope to the hopeless. Jesus announced while teaching in the temple area, "I do nothing on my own but speak just what the Father has taught me. The one who sent me is with me" (John 8:28–29). As imitators of Jesus, each of us can say, "I do nothing on my own but serve as my Lord has taught me. Jesus who sent me is with me."

To serve like Jesus served finally comes down to one thing: faith. The willingness to give everything you have and more because you know in your heart that God is the ultimate provider. The courage to risk your own comfort because you trust that God will come through, no matter how hopeless your task may appear to be. The humility to seek God's glory and not your own because you understand the true source of grace.

When I started attending New Song, I learned two things right away. The first was that this was where I belonged. The second was that this was scary! I wondered what God would ask me to give up, and I doubted whether I could actually follow through.

For example, every now and then, a family in the church would feel a call and move to some distant place to serve God. One afternoon after a young couple moved to South Africa, I stopped by Pastor Brian's office to talk about this issue.

Brian was relaxing, sitting back in his desk chair with his office door open. I took the opportunity, politely knocked, and said, "Brian, do you have a couple of minutes to talk? I have a quick question about how things work around here."

"Sure, Rick, what's going on?"

I stepped in and sat on the couch next to his desk. "I'm new to all this 'listen to God, follow Jesus' stuff, so I'm not sure how it all really works, but I am afraid that God is going to tell me to quit my job and move to South Africa. I love my job. I don't want to lose it."

Brian gave me a big grin and reassured me, "That's not quite the way God works." Then he said something prophetic. "When and if he calls you, you will be ready to go."

His phone rang, so I whispered a quick thank-you and slipped out. I would have forgotten all about that short conversation if it wasn't for something that happened later that year on a plane over the Pacific.

Six months after my meeting with Brian, my wife and I were invited to teach for two weeks at a small Bible school in the Philippines. We agreed to go in part because it was during my summer vacation, so it would not interfere with my job. It was a life-changing experience. It started when Bonnie and I arrived in Davao but our luggage didn't. After my initial frustration, I thought this must be like the time Jesus told the seventy-two in Luke 10:4, "Do not take a purse or bag or sandals." The luggage was found ten days later, but in the meantime, Bonnie and I had to do the best we could with the clothes on our backs. That turned out to be the least of our discomforts. We were tested at every turn. Even though we took precautions, we both got sick (though only for a short time). We saw poverty like we had never seen it before, and it broke our hearts. God challenged us in ways that were beyond our imaginations. We got very little sleep. We were constantly on the go, from the slums of Davao to the jungles of the Philippines.

The day before we were to leave, a man came to us and told us he was on his way to buy a gun and kill himself, but he had decided to give prayer one more chance. We were over our heads but had no choice. We prayed with him and counseled him for three hours. By the way, it worked…he left no longer wanting to kill himself.

On the flight home, I turned to my wife and said something which had been unimaginable to me just a few months earlier when I talked with Brian. "I want to quit my job and do this full-time."

Sitting on that plane, totally worn out, I realized that I had just spent two weeks working alongside Jesus. I had seen lives transformed. When I felt inadequate to the task, I had found a new strength that I never imagined possible. Instead of thinking about the sleepless nights or the uncomfortable feeling of speaking to a church in clothes I had worn for six straight days, I remembered most the day we had walked through a jungle to a pool in a small river. There, with the sound of a nearby waterfall in the background, eight members of a local village were baptized into the kingdom. After that, how could I ever go back to my old, comfortable, boring life?

Since then, I have devoted myself to working with the poor and homeless in Tacoma, the Philippines, and around the world. In the end, it may have cost me everything I thought I wanted, but the reality is it has cost me nothing.

Chapter Five

FORGIVE LIKE JESUS FORGAVE

I don't think I fully understood the importance of forgiveness until the strange events one night in the Philippines. It was my fourth evening teaching at a church in Davao. It had been an exciting week. Attendance had been growing each night as people invited their friends. This evening, the church was packed. The weather had cooled down from its usual stifling heat, so the church was comfortable. We had three excellent interpreters, and I was gaining experience in the translation process. It seemed like we were a well-oiled machine. I was looking forward to speaking that night. The topic was a favorite of mine—forgiveness. Everything was in place for a powerful evening.

It started just as I expected. Everything was going smoothly. Then, about ten minutes into my presentation, I said something that I thought was simple:

"The enemy does not want us to be forgiving because unforgiveness destroys us, while forgiveness sets us free."

I paused, waiting for Pastor Ronald to translate. Ronald had been translating for me all week without any problems. He has an excellent command of English. In those rare times when he had difficulty with a word, his daughter, Kizza, would help out.

As I waited for Ronald to translate my sentence, I realized something was wrong. He spoke a couple of words, then turned and looked back at me. Thinking he could not remember my exact phrasing, I repeated it: "The enemy does not want us to be forgiving because unforgiveness destroys us, while forgiveness sets us free."

Once again Ronald tried to translate but paused after just a few words. Kizza realized something was wrong, so she jumped in—but she could only get a couple of Cebuano words out before she shared her father's puzzled expression.

I was surprised, since translation had not been a problem during the prior three sessions. Our well-oiled machine was quickly breaking down. I decided I was the cause of the problem. I needed to rephrase the sentence.

"Satan does not want us to forgive each other. He wants us to suffer when forgiveness would set us free."

It didn't help. Neither Ronald nor Kizza could translate. For at least ten minutes I tried to come up with different ways to say the same thing, but nothing changed. I was quickly running out of possibilities and thought I might just give up when, as abruptly as it had started, the problem stopped. The translation process was once again smooth. Ronald seemed back on track. We were able to finish the lesson.

Later that evening as Ronald accompanied us back to our hotel, he asked me, "Did you notice the trouble I had translating the first part of your message?"

Somewhat embarrassed, I answered, "Sure, I was meaning to apologize to you for not making myself clear when I started."

"It wasn't your fault at all," he assured me. "It was the strangest thing. All of a sudden I couldn't translate. I could understand what you were saying, but I couldn't put it into my language. I thought I was doing something wrong until I saw that Kizza was having the same problem. Then I knew it was the enemy at work. I prayed and rebuked the enemy, and it all came back to me."

Now I understood. I told Ronald, "I guess the enemy does not want us to understand the power of forgiveness."

I was right. That night turned out to be the most powerful evening at the church. At the end of the service, I asked people to pause and ask God whom they needed to forgive. Before it was all over, a wave of forgiveness washed over the church. Over the next few days, we heard stories of healing between husbands and wives. For the first time in a long time, one of the wives was able to tell her husband, in public, that she loved him. Bad feelings that had built up over the year between students were released. Friendships were renewed, families were reunited.

That night I learned the true power of forgiveness and that the enemy will do anything to stop it. Forgiveness is one of several universal themes woven into the Bible from the beginning to the end. But of all those themes, the one that provides the most hope, the one that most defines mercy, the one that gives shape to love, is forgiveness. Without it, we would be lost forever. There would be no point to life, no purpose for our existence, no hope for the future.

In a perfect world, forgiveness is unnecessary, but in a fallen world, it is essential.

Forgiveness was always a central part of God's plan for restoring his creation. Knowing we were unable to redeem ourselves, God sent his Son to pay what we couldn't, make a way for forgiveness, and at the same time, teach us how to forgive.

WHAT IS FORGIVENESS?

Forgiveness is commonly understood to be the act of releasing someone from the consequences of an offense. Like most of what Jesus came to teach us, we tend to think we grasp the concept, but what we really know is a corrupted version of forgiveness. Forgiveness is understood on one level but practiced on another. In the abstract, the world views forgiveness as a virtue, similar to honesty, patience, and sensitivity. But while the world might label forgiveness as a virtue, it only plays lip service to the ideal.

Our true feelings about forgiveness are best reflected in the movies we watch. Hollywood produces two types of films related to forgiveness. One is the rare movie in which the villain is forgiven and eventually changes his or her ways. The other is the much more common revenge movie, where the hero deals out swift and bloody justice. We may shed a tear at the first type of movie, but we cheer at the second. Revenge taps into a primeval and visceral emotion that overpowers the virtue of forgiveness.

In theory, forgiveness includes granting a pardon, letting go of a grudge, setting aside a wrong, not demanding restitution for a loss, choosing not to be angry, and putting aside plans for revenge. Sounds good, right? But in practice, forgiveness is also letting others "off the hook," allowing them to "get away with it," permitting them to "escape the consequences of their actions," indulging "bad behavior," issuing a "get out of jail free" card. When expressed this way, forgiveness no longer sounds so noble. Instead, it sounds downright unfair and unjust.

The world melds these two opposing views together to produce a concept of forgiveness with strings attached. The strings are many and varied.

- Forgiveness can come only after a sign of remorse.
- There must be an apology before there can be forgiveness.
- The offense must be small, the harm minimal.
- The offender must be a friend.
- A penalty must first be paid.

The list goes on and on. What the world calls forgiveness is actually conditional forgiveness—a classic oxymoron. The two words do not belong together. Christian forgiveness is never conditional, otherwise it is not forgiveness.

The definition of forgiveness is the simple, straightforward act of granting someone a free pardon for any offense without any conditions. Our real problem is not with the meaning of forgiveness; it is deciding how far forgiveness should go. Even at its best, the world usually stops short of a real understanding of forgiveness. Ultimately, Jesus came to teach us something more radical than anyone ever imagined about the true reach of forgiveness.

Why Is Forgiveness Difficult?

Forgiveness, as the world defines it, is difficult because it conflicts with our sense of justice. We play a balancing game, pitting the severity of the offense against the virtue of forgiveness. Forgiveness is easy to give for a word spoken in anger, but difficult for an act of murder. The constant tug-of-war between the cry for justice and the virtue of forgiveness makes it hard to find balance. The fundamental problem is that we consider forgiveness to be an act of justice when it is really an act of love, with no relationship to justice at all.

Forgiveness is also difficult because we confuse it with rehabilitation. It is just one of many ways to change the behavior of an offender. Perhaps an offender can learn from the mercy we display and not repeat the offense. But if offenders continue to offend, our patience begins to wear thin, and we give up on forgiveness in favor of "teaching them a lesson"—for their own good, I might add.

The fundamental problem here is that true forgiveness is not a tool of rehabilitation. Though it has the potential to change an offender's behavior, the focus of forgiveness should be on the changes it produces in the life of the victim, not of the perpetrator.

How Did Jesus Forgive?

Jesus's whole life was a lesson in forgiveness. The plans of God, forged in the garden as he confronted Adam and Eve, were to be fulfilled in the death of Jesus on the cross. But Christ's death was not the beginning of forgiveness. It was the culmination of a long work of God's forgiveness that was accomplished when Jesus, with his last breath, proclaimed from the cross, "It is finished."

Jesus did more than complete God's plan of forgiveness and thereby open the door to redemption and restoration. He also taught us the importance of forgiveness in our relationships on earth. He showed us how to forgive each other. He warned us about the dangers of unforgiveness. He introduced us to the power of forgiveness. He laid the foundation for living a life of forgiveness in five principles:

- Forgiveness is a command.
- Forgiveness is difficult.
- Forgiveness is not conditional.
- Unforgiveness will destroy us.
- Forgiveness has power.

PRINCIPLE 1: FORGIVENESS IS A COMMAND

This command, if not followed, has frightening consequences. Nowhere is this made clearer than in the parable of the unforgiving servant found in Matthew 18:23–25:

> Therefore, the kingdom of heaven is like a king who wanted to settle accounts with his servants. As he began the settlement, a man who owed him ten thousand talents was brought to him. Since he was not able to pay, the master ordered that he and his wife and his children and all that he had be sold to repay the debt.
>
> The servant fell on his knees before him. "Be patient with me," he begged, "and I will pay back everything." The servant's master took pity on him, canceled the debt and let him go.
>
> But when that servant went out, he found one of his fellow servants who owed him a hundred denarii. He grabbed him and began to choke him. "Pay back what you owe me!" he demanded.
>
> His fellow servant fell to his knees and begged him, "Be patient with me, and I will pay you back." But he refused. Instead, he went off and had the man thrown into prison until he could pay the debt. When the other servants saw what had happened, they were greatly distressed and went and told their master everything that had happened.
>
> Then the master called the servant in. "You wicked servant," he said, "I canceled all that debt of yours because you begged me to. Shouldn't you have had mercy on your fellow servant just as I had on you?" In anger his master turned him over to the jailers to be tortured, until he should pay back all he owed.
>
> This is how my heavenly Father will treat each of you unless you forgive your brother from your heart.

This may seem like a harsh response from the master, but it is totally just. Consider the behavior of the servant. He knew his debt was great and cried out for mercy from the master. But when the servant was owed a debt, he focused on what he would lose if the debt wasn't paid. He lost sight of everything the master had sacrificed to forgive his own debt. We must not lose sight of the price God paid to forgive our debt! The sacrifice of his Son reflects our worth to him.

Jesus repeated the command to forgive several other times. Each time it came with the same warning: if the command is not followed, the Father will not forgive us. He taught this to the disciples in Mark 11:25: "And when you stand praying, if you hold anything against anyone, forgive him, so that your Father in heaven may forgive you your sins." And he repeated this command while teaching the disciples how to pray in Matthew 6:14–15: "For if you forgive men when they sin against you, your heavenly Father will also forgive you. But if you do not forgive men their sins, your Father will not forgive your sins."

PRINCIPLE 2: FORGIVENESS IS DIFFICULT

We associate forgiveness with justice, but God associates forgiveness with love. True forgiveness is not an act of justice. It is an act of love. A judge has many options in the determination of guilt and punishment, but forgiveness is not one of them. Forgiveness is not a judicial action. On the other hand, it is a *requirement* of love. If we are to love our enemies, then our love begins with our forgiving them. If we can learn to separate the concepts of justice and forgiveness, we can better accept our responsibly to forgive.

On our first mission visit to the Philippines, I learned how tough it can be to forgive. One day my wife and I were praying for a young lady named Maela. Maela spoke some English, but we had an interpreter to make sure she fully understood the prayer time. While we were praying, God told me to stop and tell Maela he loved her and that she was a princess in his kingdom. As soon as she heard this, Maela started to cry. The interpreter told us that we had no idea how much that meant to her. Once she told us Maela's story, we understood.

From the beginning, her mother had never wanted her. She had actually tried to abort her. Obviously, the abortion failed, but it left

Maela with a slight disability in her left hand which serves as a constant reminder of her mother's rejection. Shortly after she was born, her mother left. Maela's father remarried, and her stepmother favored her own daughters. By the time Maela was fourteen, her stepmother had convinced her father to kick her out into the streets. She has lived with friends and other family members ever since. The experience left her more than just feeling unloved: she was convinced she was unlovable. Even God couldn't love her.

When I told her God loved her dearly, it was hard for her to believe, but it was just what she needed to hear. For the rest of the week, Bonnie and I poured love on Maela. We prayed with her several times and reached the point where we started to encourage her to forgive her parents. We knew that was a tall order. She had never experienced a moment of love or compassion from them. They had never expressed any regret for their treatment of her, much less repented. Yet we knew Maela still had a spark of love for her father, because she told us the one thing she wanted most in the world was a birthday card from him. We were not surprised that she was unwilling to forgive them at first. That was okay, because we understood, and we knew God would give her the strength to forgive one day. We continued to pray with her. By the time we left, she told us that she was, for the first time in her life, willing to consider forgiving her parents.

PRINCIPLE 3: FORGIVENESS IS NOT CONDITIONAL

Just as the disciples recognized that Jesus prayed in a unique way, they also saw that he was more open in his approach to forgiveness than anyone they had seen. The disciples recognized that Jesus was a polarizing figure in Israel. They saw the times when people flocked to him, honored him, and praised him. They also saw the times when he was ridiculed, rejected, and despised. They must have marveled at his response to the hate directed toward him. Even when the people of his own hometown took offense at him, he did not respond in kind. He quietly reflected on the meaning of their rejection as he went on with his business.

Trying to understand all this, Peter asked Jesus about possible conditions on forgiveness, saying, "Lord, how many times shall I forgive my brother when he sins against me? Up to seven times?" (Matthew 18:21). As usual, Peter thought he had figured this out on his own. I'm sure, in Peter's mind, forgiving seven times displayed a godly level of patience! Jesus made it clear in the next verse, however, that there is no condition on the number of times we are called to forgive.

"Jesus answered, 'I tell you, not seven times, but seventy times seven'" (Matthew 18:22). By this, Jesus did not mean that 490 offenses are the boundary of forgiveness. Just as today the expression "No, a thousand times no" means never, seventy times seven means there is no limit.

What Jesus doesn't say about forgiveness is almost as important and shocking as what he does say. He does not instruct us to evaluate the sincerity of the repentance. You would think that after the third time in the same day you hear the same claim of "I'm sorry, I will never do that again," it would be time to roll your eyes and say, "I have already heard that twice today; how can I believe you now?" But that is not the command. Jesus said nothing about the nature of the repentance, just that our response should always be, "You are forgiven." We are to forgive every offense as often as it occurs without consideration of the sincerity of any act of repentance.

Perhaps the best picture of unconditional forgiveness was modeled by Jesus as he was hanging from the cross. His words are recorded in Luke 23:34: "Father, forgive them, for they do not know what they are doing." Jesus spoke these words while he was in agony. The people he forgave were not on their knees asking for forgiveness or in any way trying to make up for what they had done. At the time he forgave them, they were cursing him, mocking him, and crying out for his blood. They continued to do so even after he forgave them. He didn't wait until he returned in his resurrected body, free of pain and triumphant. He forgave them on the spot. Forgiveness is not to be postponed until the hurt goes away. The quiet lesson Jesus taught us all on that dark night is that forgiveness does not require repentance, nor does it wait for things to turn out all right.

If we are to forgive like Jesus forgave, we can never withhold it. We cannot put conditions on it. We cannot claim that we have been forgiving enough but have been pushed too far to continue. We cannot hold out until there is an apology. Forgiveness is a command we must follow if we are to be forgiven by the Father.

Jesus displayed a degree of forgiveness that was totally unconditional. From the snubs and sneers of the Pharisees to the nails pounded into his wrists, he responded with forgiveness. How can we do less?

PRINCIPLE 4: UNFORGIVENESS WILL DESTROY US

Forgiveness can be difficult, especially when an offense is too egregious for us to overlook. Either the pain runs too deep for us to find comfort, or the offenders are far too callous to realize how much they have hurt us. The thought of forgiveness under such circumstances not only reeks of injustice, it intensifies the pain. Revenge and retribution appear to be the only way to calm the storm in our minds. In such a circumstance, we become consumed by the rage of unforgiveness. Our anger turns to bitterness, bitterness to malice, and the mind begins to rot with hatred.

But unforgiveness will not change the circumstances of your pain. Vengeance will not restore what was lost. It will, however, change you in an ugly way. It will rob you of peace. It will deliver you into the hands of the enemy.

Paul warned about uncontrolled anger in Ephesians 4:26: "In your anger do not sin. Do not let the sun go down while you are still angry." In the next verse he explained why this was so important. Anger that is unchecked by forgiveness "[gives] a foothold to the devil" (Ephesians 4:27).

In the midst of a terrible loss, we may believe forgiveness is a sign of weakness, allowing the offender to get away with inflicting great pain. Yet, far from allowing evil to succeed, forgiveness actually foils the schemes of the enemy. God wants us to be forgiving; the enemy wants us to hold a grudge. God wants us to be loving; the enemy wants us to be filled with hate.

Paul exposed the enemy when he wrote to the Corinthian church, "If you forgive anyone, I also forgive him. And what I have forgiven—if there was anything to forgive—I have forgiven in the sight of Christ for your sake, *in order that Satan might not outwit us. For we are not unaware of his schemes"* (2 Corinthians 2:10–11). In the Greek, Paul's warning is even more powerful. It really means "that Satan might not gain an advantage over us." If the enemy schemes to promote unforgiveness, it is for one reason. He wants a foothold in our lives. He uses our anger and our bitterness to lead us into sin.

Unforgiveness allows the sin of others to change us. We become defined by their transgressions. It leaves us stuck in a perpetual cycle of pain. The enemy uses our unforgiveness to create confusion, hate, bitterness, and defeat. We may rage against evil forged in the fire of injustice, but in the process, we are consumed by it as well. Either we begin to believe we are unworthy and deserve the pain or we become embittered by the injustice.

This was true of Maela. The pain of her parents' rejection went far deeper than the pain in her damaged hand. It changed what she thought of herself. Maela believed she was unlovable because those who should have loved her the most had rejected her. It eventually led her to believe the lie of the enemy that even God did not love her. Her damaged hand could be healed more easily than her wounded soul.

Unforgiveness can even lead us into becoming the instruments of injustice. Hollywood may teach that revenge is the cure for injustice, but it isn't. The drive to gain revenge only spirals out of control, hurting us and those we love as much or more than those who hurt us in the first place. One act of vengeance inevitably leads to another act of vengeance. Without forgiveness, vengeance never finds rest.

Perhaps even more tragic is that when we are unable to forgive, we are also unable to help those who have also become victims. As long as we are consumed by our own pain, there is no room for the pain of others. If we are bent on revenge, there is no place in our lives to dispense comfort.

David understood this. He saw it played out in his hometown, Ziklag. He and his men had just returned home, only to discover that it had been sacked in their absence. Their sons and daughters had been killed or taken off into captivity. Their pain ran deep: "So David and his men wept aloud until they had no strength left to weep" (1 Samuel 30:4). But in the end, David's reaction was different from his men's. His men became "bitter in spirit" and wanted revenge not only against their enemy but against David as well, because he had allowed their city to be left unprotected. David, however, "found strength in the LORD his God" (1 Samuel 30:6). David would later write about his understanding of forgiveness in Psalm 71:20: "Though you have made me see troubles, many and bitter, you will restore my life again; from the depths of the earth you will again bring me up." Life is hard. We will be hurt by strangers and friends. Vengeance will never help, but God provides peace.

All unforgiveness offers us is a life of bitterness while opening a foothold the enemy will exploit. It promises to restore balance, to allow us to get even with those who hurt us, but it only sucks us into a black hole of sin. As Jesus taught, and as David discovered, we need to find our strength in the Lord, not in our desire for revenge.

PRINCIPLE 5: FORGIVENESS HAS POWER

As I prayed for a woman in church one day, she told me she had been a drug user for many years. She had been clean for almost a year since she found Jesus, but she had contracted hepatitis while she was using. She wanted prayer for healing.

As I prayed for her, God said she was healed because she had never used drugs. No drugs, no hepatitis. I wondered what he meant, so I silently asked him. He told me that when she asked for forgiveness, he not only forgave her, he changed her past.

I learned that day that godly forgiveness has the power to change what can't be changed. Forgiveness does more than heal the past and all its hurts. It erases it. Forgiveness restores your innocence.

Maela eventually forgave her parents, and in doing so, she acknowledged that they were the ones who were damaged, not her. They became the ones who needed love and compassion. Maela eliminated the advantage the enemy had over her and now is in a place where she can help her parents and others. She became free to be all God intended her to be.

Forgiveness has even more power than I could ever imagine, as God taught me once as I prepared a message for Sunday morning. God directed my attention to Matthew 5:48: "Be perfect, therefore, as your heavenly Father is perfect." It is a command that made little sense to me. How could I be perfect? It sounded sacrilegious even to consider the possibility. Yet there it was in black and white—Jesus commanding us to be perfect. I knew Jesus was not in the habit of issuing commands we cannot obey. Jesus came to teach us how we should live in this world, and evidently, that includes being perfect.

It was a real puzzle for me, but since God had directed me to the verse, I asked him, "What does this verse mean, and what do you want me to say about it Sunday?" His answer shocked me. It completely changed my concept of forgiveness. In one simple sentence he made it all clear:

"Don't you know that being forgiven is the same thing as being perfect?"

I hadn't known that, but it suddenly made sense.

There is an old Christian bumper sticker I rarely see anymore. It says, "Christians aren't perfect, they are just forgiven." I had always thought that was cute, but now I know it is wrong. It should read, "Christians are perfect *because* they are forgiven." I would not go around with that on my bumper because it would be misunderstood, yet that is exactly the essence of Jesus's command. Once you are forgiven, you are restored to a state of perfection in the eyes of the Lord. Your past is rewritten.

The writer of Hebrews, understanding what Jesus meant, observed that, "By one sacrifice he has made perfect forever those who are being made holy" (Hebrews 10:14). To obey this seemingly impossible command, do one thing—seek forgiveness. To gain forgiveness, you have to give it as well. Jesus commanded us to forgive by teaching us the final and greatest reward of forgiveness: the restoration of perfection. Such is the ultimate power of forgiveness.

How Should We Forgive?

We are called to imitate Jesus in all things, including forgiveness. Paul made this clear in Colossians 3:13–14: "Bear with each other and forgive whatever grievances you may have against one another. *Forgive as the Lord forgave you."* The command is clear. The power of forgiveness is evident. The model of Jesus stands as our goal. Our response should be simple: forgive others as God has forgiven us.

Forgiveness begins by being "slow to anger." There is little to forgive where there is no offense taken. As James explained, "Everyone should be quick to listen, slow to speak and slow to become angry; for man's anger does not bring about the righteousness of God" (James 1:20).

We are to imitate Jesus, who did only what he saw his father doing. In that sense, Jesus was the embodiment of what David wrote in Psalm 103:8–10: "The Lord is compassionate and gracious, slow to anger, abounding in love. He will not always accuse, nor will he harbor his anger forever; he does not treat us as our sins deserve or repay us according to our iniquities."

Such forgiveness requires supernatural strength. It was the presence of the Holy Spirit in Jesus that allowed him to see beyond his pain to the heart of God, finding the strength to forgive. When Jesus taught that we are to forgive over and over again, the apostles did not argue the impracticality, the unfairness, or the injustice of it all. Instead, they realized that what Jesus asked was impossible in the natural world, so their only response was, "Increase our faith!" (Luke 17:5).

The apostles recognized that the key to how we should forgive is supernatural power. It is the kind of power that comes through the Holy Spirit. Jesus said as much in John 20:18: "Receive the Holy Spirit. If you forgive anyone his sins, they are forgiven; if you do not forgive them, they are not forgiven." The second sentence makes no sense without the first sentence. In our own strength, we do not have the power or the authority to decide who will be forgiven and who will not. But filled with the Holy Spirit and resting in him, we have the strength to forgive. Only the presence of the Holy Spirit gives us the wisdom to understand forgiveness and the authority and will to forgive in the way Jesus taught.

Forgiveness is hard because the need to forgive implies the existence of an injury. Our typical response to pain is to run away from it, just as our hand jerks away from a hot stove. We want the source of our pain to go away, but forgiveness requires us to walk into our pain and acknowledge it. We are asked to confront the source of our pain, not with anger but with love. That's why it so hard to forgive and so easy to hate. That is why those who forgive stand out. Some are able to forgive a few people who have hurt them. Few can forgive every hurt.

Here are a few suggestions that will make it easier to forgive:

- Allow God to be your strength; turn to him for comfort.
- Allow faith, not bitterness, to rule in your life.
- Be quick to forgive, because allowing a hurt to fester only makes forgiveness more difficult.
- Do not expect nor wait for an apology or acknowledgment of your condition.

You can be among those few who stand out in the world because they forgave like Jesus did. You can do it because the Holy Spirit is in you, just as he was in Jesus. Allow the Holy Spirit to change your perspective and see your tormentor as tormented, your oppressor as oppressed, your pain as shared. It is one of the mysteries of the universe that pain which runs deep will not heal through the infliction of more pain on someone else. Such agony can only be redeemed by the tender release of mercy and forgiveness.

Chapter Six

ENCOURAGE LIKE JESUS ENCOURAGED

One Thursday, I arrived at our evening church service a little early. I took a seat near the front. As usual I had my cell phone with me, so I checked to make sure it was on vibrate. Then I did something I never do before church: I looked at my old messages. As I scrolled through them, I saw one from my friend Brent that I had not deleted.

Something about seeing his name caught my attention—it was almost like it flashed at me. I felt a strong urge to call him. I never make calls like that just before church, but this time I felt it was necessary, though I had no idea why. Phone in hand, I left my seat and walked to the back of the church. As I went out the door, I dialed Brent. The phone rang several times. Just as I was about to give up and go back to the service, Brent answered.

"Brent, this is Rick, how are you doing?"

There was a long pause.

"Brent, are you still there?"

Brent finally answered, "I can't believe you called just now."

I knew Brent was going through some tough times, and I had tried to make myself available to talk with him whenever he needed it. So my immediate thought was that something terrible must have happened. I explained, "I was sitting in church waiting for it to start and felt like I had to call you."

Brent answered, "I can't believe this! I have been on my knees praying for the last forty-five minutes. I just asked God to send someone to talk to when I heard the phone ring."

I was late for church that evening because I spent the next half hour talking to Brent. Just before I hung up, he said, "I can't believe God did this. I was feeling so down and alone, but now I am so encouraged."

That night, I learned the power of encouragement.

As I write this in February 2011, it is two weeks before the Green Bay vs. Pittsburgh Super Bowl. How do you think the coaches are preparing their teams? Are they going into detail over every botched play of the season, accusing each player of messing up, warning them that if they do that in the big game, they will lose? Or are they reminding them of the exceptional plays made during the season, telling them that when they play like that, they will certainly win?

It may be a mixture of both, but I believe it is in our nature to respond better to encouragement than to criticism. God didn't start things out with Adam by saying, "I'm watching you, don't blow it." No, the first thing God did after he created man was to speak words of encouragement: "God blessed them" (Genesis 1:28). Realizing the importance of sharing both successes and burdens, God also gave Adam a helpmate to, among other things, encourage him. The Hebrew word used to describe Eve, often translated as "helper," means to surround, to succor, or to be of assistance, especially in times of trouble. That exactly defines encouragement: stepping in and helping out when needed.

Eve was created to encourage Adam. Her role was to cheer him on when he did things right and comfort him when things went wrong. Adam had the corresponding responsibility to encourage Eve.

Ever since, encouragement has been such an important part of life that all of us have either experienced its blessing or longed for it when it was withheld. Nothing can lift someone's spirits like a simple pat on the back and a "Well done." On the other hand, nothing can sap someone's strength like being criticized—or worse, ignored. The American author and pastor William Ward put it this way: "Flatter me, and I may not believe you. Criticize me, and I may not like you. Ignore me, and I may not forgive you. Encourage me, and I will not forget you."

When Jesus came, he not only taught us how to encourage others, he shared our human need to be encouraged. Nowhere was that more clearly demonstrated than on the day he was arrested. That night, while he prayed about his coming death, he asked for the support of Peter, James, and John: "He began to be deeply distressed and troubled. 'My soul is overwhelmed with sorrow to the point of death,' he said to them. 'Stay here and keep watch'" (Mark 14:33–34). At that moment, he needed his friends to have his back, to comfort and support him, to encourage him as he walked though the terrible events of the next few days. Even though they did not understand what was to come, all Jesus wanted was his friends by his side.

In the Luke version of the story, God sent an angel to strengthen Jesus, but even that was not enough. Jesus needed the encouragement of his friends on earth. That need stands as one more testimony to his humanity.

But sadly, he returned to find the disciples sleeping. He asked them, "Could you men not keep watch with me for one hour?" (Matthew 26:40). Read Jesus's words carefully. Feel the deep disappointment of one abandoned by his friends at the most critical time in his life. I believe the pain of discouragement at that moment exceeded even the pain of the betrayal which was to come when the disciples scattered during his trial. Encouragement was the first need of Adam that God supplied; the withholding of encouragement was the first intensely personal loss Jesus experienced on his road to the cross.

Jesus understood our need to be encouraged. He knew the power of words to lift us up or bring us down. Even he was not immune to their power. So he came to teach us how to comfort those in need, how to bless those who achieve greatness, and how to draw the best out of people by encouraging them.

What Is Encouragement?

Encouragement is the process of breathing courage into another. In its simplest form, encouragement is the act of pointing someone in the right direction—showing him or her the path from despair to hope, from failure to success, from resignation to reaffirmation.

Encouragement also points the oppressed to the outstretched hand of God. It leads the rejected to their true worth. It directs the fearful to the promise of their future. It guides the hopeless to their full potential. Perhaps the best definition is that encouragement is the process of changing someone's focus away from the lies of the enemy to the truth of God's plan.

Like so much of what Jesus modeled for us, encouragement is a command. It is found throughout the Bible, including in Isaiah 1:16–17: "Stop doing wrong, learn to do right! Seek justice, *encourage* the oppressed. Defend the cause of the fatherless, plead the case of the widow." Lest we minimize the importance of encouragement, notice the context in the passage from Isaiah. Encouragement is listed along with seeking justice, doing right, and defending the weak.

In the New Testament, the command to encourage is found in Hebrews 10:25: "Let us not give up meeting together, as some are in the habit of doing, but let us *encourage one another*—and all the more as you see the Day approaching." Once again, the context is important. "The Day" refers to the day of judgment. Encouragement takes on special significance as trials and tribulations increase. Encouragement is necessary as the pressure of the enemy increases. Encouragement is a powerful weapon against the enemy's lies: "*Encourage* one another daily, as long as it is called Today, so that none of you may be hardened by sin's deceitfulness" (Hebrews 3:13–14).

Since the enemy lies to us daily, encouragement should be an important part of our daily defense strategy. Without it we could become hardened to the truth. It's that important. Withholding encouragement strengthens the lies of the enemy to the point at which encouragement no longer helps. Discouragement can paralyze us. When discouraged, we feel like we are walking through wet concrete. Every step forward is weighted down and difficult. When it is first laid, wet concrete can easily be shoveled out. But when the concrete hardens, it takes a jackhammer to loosen it. We cannot allow the lies of Satan to take a foothold in the lives of those we love.

Paul recognized the importance of encouragement to the body when he wrote to the Thessalonian church, "Encourage one another and build each other up" (1 Thessalonians 5:11). As Paul saw it, encouragement is a necessary tool in the effort to build up a strong, bold body of Christ.

How Jesus Encouraged Others

Just as love and service are connected, service and encouragement share a common bond. Service typically comes in the form of actions; encouragement often comes in the form of words. The two complement each other, merging together as they did so often in the life of Jesus.

When the centurion came to Jesus, asking him to heal his servant, Jesus first spoke words of encouragement as he announced to the disciples, "I have not found anyone in Israel with such great faith" (Matthew 8:10). Jesus followed this encouragement with an act of service by healing the servant. Despite this connection, his words of encouragement are sometimes lost in light of the amazing miracles he performed. But those words of encouragement are just as important as the miracles.

Focusing on the words of Jesus reveals at least four ways he encouraged the people he touched: he pointed them to their worth, he pointed them to their future, he pointed them to their strengths, and he pointed them to God.

Jesus Pointed Others to Their Worth

The poor, the oppressed, and the disheartened generally feel left out. They know the pain of rejection. They feel worthless. But God does not reject them. He knows their worth and encourages them. David wrote in Psalm 10:17, "You hear, O LORD, the desire of the afflicted; you encourage them, and you listen to their cry." Jesus brought that quality of God with him when he came to earth. He made a point of spending time with the poor and the downtrodden. As a result, he made them feel loved and worthy. When the enemy whispered in their ears, "You have nothing, you are nothing," Jesus countered with the truth: "I want to be near you, because you are worth more to me than you can imagine."

When John the Baptist asked if Jesus was the promised Messiah, Jesus offered this as evidence for who he was: "The good news is preached to the poor" (Matthew 11:5). The word Jesus used for "poor" is an alternative word for "beggar." According to Jesus, part of the evidence that he was the Son of God was that his ministry included the man dressed in dirty, tattered rags, begging in the streets.

While having dinner in the home of a prominent Pharisee, Jesus said, "But when you give a banquet, invite the poor, the crippled, the lame, the blind, and you will be blessed" (Luke 14:13–14). The blessing is not that God will give you a gold star for associating with the poor. The blessing is that you will discover the worth of those who have been rejected.

Jesus was inclusive. He left no one out. Everyone had worth. He was just as likely to be at a poor man's home as he was to be in the home of a Pharisee. He allowed a prostitute to wash his feet with her hair. He visited the home of the chief tax gatherer in Jericho. From the beggar in the street to the rich man in his home, they all had worth in his eyes.

Even the lowest of the lowest in society were worthy of Jesus's attention. No better example can be found than when Jesus did something unheard of in his time. The story is found in Matthew 8:1–3:

> When he came down from the mountainside, large crowds followed him. A man with leprosy came and knelt before him and said, "Lord, if you are willing, you can make me clean." Jesus reached out his hand and touched the man. "I am willing," he said. "Be clean!" Immediately he was cured of his leprosy.

Everything that happened in this story was socially unacceptable. First, the man with leprosy approached and knelt before Jesus. Totally inappropriate! Lepers were not allowed to approach anyone. They were branded with a disease that forced them to remain isolated. Second, the leper spoke to Jesus. Lepers were only allowed to cry out from a distance, "Unclean, unclean." Any other conversation with a leper was forbidden. Yet, Jesus did not respond with shock or horror to this egregious breach of social norms. Instead, in the ultimate act of mercy and compassion, Jesus healed the man. But the miracle of healing is not the most surprising part of this story. The surprising part is that he reached out his hand and touched him. Even if the man had not been healed, his life would have been transformed by that touch. He had probably not felt a gentle, caring human touch for years. By touching him, Jesus announced that he had worth.

In another powerful encounter, Jesus's words of encouragement were nearly overshadowed by a miracle of healing. I'm referring to the story of the woman who had a bleeding disorder, told in Matthew 9:20–22. For twelve years this woman had sought help for her plight but found nothing. Like so many of the chronically ill, she had probably been told it was her fault. Chronic illness is often viewed as God's punishment on the unworthy. From her actions, it is likely that she had come to the point where she felt she deserved her illness and was not worthy of healing. She was not even worthy of facing Jesus to ask for healing as so many other sick people had done. She reasoned, "If I can only sneak up behind him and just touch his cloak, I will be healed." This is exactly what she did. At that moment, Jesus turned to her, looked her in the eye, and said, "Take heart, daughter…your faith has healed you" (Matthew 9:22). In an instant, twelve years of lies melted away. She *was* worthy of a face-to-face encounter with Jesus. She was a daughter of Christ. And most important of all, her faith had healed her. She had something of worth.

The phrase used by Jesus here, translated "take heart," really means "have courage." With a word, Jesus literally breathed courage *and* healing into this woman. She had come to him broken, sick, and unworthy. She left not only healed, but with the knowledge that she was worthy.

The power of this kind of encouragement is limitless. We are drawn to those who recognize our worth. This was demonstrated early in the ministry of Jesus in the town of Capernaum. When it was time for Jesus to move on, the people didn't want him to leave. The story is told in Luke 4:42: "The people were looking for him and when they came to where he was, they tried to keep him from leaving them." The word translated "looking" more literally means "craving." They couldn't get enough of him. They never wanted him to leave. Think about it in your own life. Aren't you drawn to people who recognize your worth? Such is the power of encouragement as Jesus lived it.

Jesus Pointed Others to Their Future

No matter what we may be going through, no matter how difficult the challenges that lay ahead, it is comforting to know our friends will walk through them with us. Jesus was looking for this on the night he was arrested. He wanted Peter, John, and James at his side. He didn't get the kind of encouragement he needed then, but he gave it throughout his life. In one of his last messages, Jesus told the disciples they were to go to the nations. Now, this could have been a frightening, imposing assignment, but he offered them this encouragement: "And surely I am with you always, to the very end of the age" (Matthew 28:20). No matter what they might face in the future, the promise was that he would be there.

Jesus kept that promise even after he ascended into heaven. When Paul was in Corinth, things began to look bad for him. It was clear he was about to be arrested. Jesus appeared to Paul in a vision, saying, "Do not be afraid; keep on speaking, do not be silent. For I am with you, and no one is going to attack and harm you" (Acts 18:9–10). I am certain that those words gave Paul the strength to continue. Paul was arrested, but just as Jesus had said, the case was thrown out of court and he was free to spend time in Corinth.

As the time drew near for Jesus to die, he prepared the disciples, encouraging them by pointing to a bright future. He told them, "Now is the time of grief, but I will see you again and you will rejoice, and no one will take away your joy" (John 16:22). I'm sure that over the three days between his death and resurrection, when all seemed lost, the disciples found comfort in those reassuring words.

This same pattern of pointing to the future is found in the Beatitudes, a kind of New Testament psalm. Jesus pointed the poor to their future, where "theirs is the kingdom of heaven" (Matthew 5:3). He reassured the grieving, telling them that "they will be comforted" (Matthew 5:4). For those who were persecuted, Jesus pointed to their reward in heaven. "Blessed are you when people insult you, persecute you and falsely say all kinds of evil against you because of me. Rejoice and be glad, because great is your reward in heaven" (Matthew 5:11–12).

Jesus consistently encouraged those who were suffering by changing their focus from their immediate pain to the promise of a better future. He understood the power of focusing on the future, because that is what he did as he faced the cross. "Let us fix our eyes on Jesus, the author and perfecter of our faith, *who for the joy set before him endured the cross,* scorning its shame, and sat down at the right hand of the throne of God" (Hebrews 12:2). The assurance of a better future encourages us to endure the present.

JESUS POINTED OTHERS TO THEIR STRENGTHS

Sometimes, when we don't have an immediate problem, we just need to know we are doing the right thing. Doubts arise because we are our own worst critics; we know our own failings all too well. The enemy is adept at exploiting our self-criticism to sow further seeds of doubt. He wants us to question our abilities, stifle our boldness, and force us to draw inward. He wants to rob us of all God intended us to be. The enemy stands ready to remind us of our sinful nature. He will tell us we are not capable of doing the right thing. Even when we do something right, he will minimize it, telling us it is not enough.

On the other hand, Jesus is always ready to celebrate our successes. He will point to our achievements, telling us, "Well done, good and faithful servant." He does so even though he is fully aware of our sins.

When a woman brought Jesus expensive perfume, the disciples thought it was a waste of money. Yet, Jesus praised and encouraged her, saying, "She has done a beautiful thing to me" (Matthew 26:10). He even said that her action would be remembered whenever the gospel was preached. What an encouragement!

When an expert in the law saw the wisdom of the teachings of Jesus, Jesus encouraged him, saying, "You are not far from the kingdom of God" (Mark 12:34). When the prostitute washed Jesus's feet with her tears, Jesus encouraged her, saying, "For she loved much" (Luke 7:47). These were all sinners. Jesus knew, down to the last detail, how much they, like all of us, had failed God. Yet Jesus chose not to bring up their past deeds as filthy rags. Instead, he encouraged and praised them for what they did right.

Perhaps there is no better example of how Jesus encouraged others with praise than the story of Zacchaeus. Zacchaeus was a wealthy tax collector in Jericho. He had become wealthy because he cheated people. When Jesus came to town, Zacchaeus, being a short man, climbed a tree to watch him. Jesus saw him in the tree and called out to him, expressing a desire to dine with him at his home. Zacchaeus was more than happy to have Jesus join him. Given his position in the town, he was not used to having guests who actually wanted to be with him! The reaction of the rest of the town was immediate and brutal: "He has gone to be the guest of a 'sinner'" (Luke 19:7).

In spite of the reaction of the crowd, Zacchaeus was encouraged by the honor Jesus paid him. During dinner, he promised to help the poor and make restitution to those he had cheated. Jesus did not respond by saying, "It's about time you turned from your sinful ways" or "Good, and don't fall back into your cheating behavior ever again." He did not highlight Zacchaeus's past weaknesses and thereby minimize what Zacchaeus had pledged to do. Instead, as he often did, Jesus praised Zacchaeus, saying, "Today salvation has come to this house, because this man, too, is a son of Abraham" (Luke 19:9). Jesus pointed Zacchaeus to his strength.

Jesus did more than encourage others by acknowledging their successes; he pointed them to their hidden strengths, their potential. Jesus was a master at inspiration, in part because he saw people not as they were, but as they could be. Peter, for example, needed to be inspired more than the other disciples because he messed up so often. When Peter recognized Jesus as the Christ, Jesus blessed him, changed his name from Simon to Peter, and said, "On this rock I will build my church" (Matthew 16:18). Later, in spite of the fact that Peter had denied him three times, Jesus encouraged Peter by reaffirming his potential, telling him to "Feed my sheep" (John 21:20). Peter's transformation from the bumbling disciple to the powerful leader of the church stands as a testimony to the ability of Jesus to encourage people to achieve greatness.

Jesus Pointed Others to God

In 1 Thessalonians 4:13–18, Paul described the coming of the Lord. He ended his discourse with words that shout with encouragement: "And so we will be with the Lord forever. Therefore encourage each other with these words." Paul understood that the words "we will be with the Lord forever" have the power to encourage future generations of believers. He had learned from Jesus that, no matter what may be going on in our lives, the ultimate encouragement is to point others toward God. When our focus is on him, our trials on earth become bearable.

Jesus lived by this truth. When tempted to turn the stones to bread during his forty-day fast, Jesus answered Satan, "Man does not live on bread alone, but on every word that comes from the mouth of God" (Matthew 3:4). Though Jesus was suffering from hunger, he found sustenance in the Word of God.

There was a time when Jesus explained to the disciples the difficulty of finding salvation: "It is easier for a camel to go through the eye of a needle than for a rich man to enter the kingdom of God" (Matthew 19:24). This disturbed the disciples. They wondered how anyone could ever be saved. Jesus both reassured and encouraged them in Matthew 19:26: "With man this is impossible, but with God all things are possible."

His answer went way beyond the boundaries of the disciples' question. It stands as a constant encouragement to all who are suffering or questioning their lives. Pointing to God with the words "with God all things are possible" has become an all-inclusive source of encouragement.

The story of Bartimaeus found in Mark 10:46–52 is another illustration of how Jesus encouraged someone by calling him to God. Bartimaeus was a blind man who begged by the road. One day as Jesus walked by, Bartimaeus, knowing the power of Jesus, began to cry out for mercy. The crowd following Jesus tried to shut him up. Surely, Jesus had more important things to do than stop for every beggar on the road! But Bartimaeus understood something they didn't. Jesus had time for everyone in need. The admonishment of the crowd only intensified his plea.

When Jesus heard Bartimaeus, he stopped. Much to the surprise of everyone (except Bartimaeus), Jesus told the disciples to bring the blind man to him. Those familiar with the story know that a miracle happened that day. Bartimaeus was healed. Yet we often miss an equally important transformation. The same crowd that had just rebuked Bartimaeus for crying out to Jesus suddenly realized something important about our Lord. "So they called to the blind man, 'Cheer up! On your feet! He's calling you'" (Mark 10:49). The phrase often translated as "cheer up" literally means "take courage" or "be encouraged." That afternoon marked the beginning of what is now the universal call of Jesus Christ to all of us: "Be encouraged, stand up, the Lord Jesus is calling you."

How Should We Encourage Others?

Encouragement involves applauding people when they do something right, comforting them when things go wrong, inspiring to them do better, and reassuring them when doubts take over. That's what Jesus did. That is what we are commanded to do.

For us, encouragement begins by spending time with people like Jesus did, showing them their worth. You cannot encourage someone unless you are willing to be with him or her. The command to encourage one another in Hebrews 10:25 comes with a precondition that makes this clear: "Let us not give up meeting together."

In my work with people on the streets, I have discovered that it doesn't take much to encourage them. Being willing to sit and talk with them, joke with them, and listen to their concerns is a great encouragement. They are so accustomed to rejection, disdainful looks, criticism, and avoidance that when someone shows even a little interest, they feel validated.

Not only have I seen the power that investing time can have in someone's life, I have also seen the damage that results from rejection and discouragement. Sadly, not all the street people who arrive early for the Sunday morning breakfast at my church choose to attend our service. Some prefer to sit outside in the elements waiting for the serving hall to open. There are a number of reasons why they choose to stay outside or sit on a hard floor by the door rather than attend church, but the one I most frequently hear is, "Church has nothing to offer me. The last church

I went to didn't seem interested in having me around, so I'm not interested in them."

This is not the kind of church Jesus came to build. While on earth, he showed interest in everyone. He wanted to be among people, and people wanted to be around him. They never would have avoided his presence in favor of a long, cold wait outside. People felt loved when he was near. Like the time Jesus touched the leper, I have found that reaching out and putting a hand on the shoulder of a homeless person has power.

Encourage others by reassuring them. Just as Jesus did, point people to their future. Tell them this time will pass, but until it does, you will stand by them. You may feel inadequate. You may not know the right words to say. That's okay. Sometimes encouraging words are spoken in silence. This is the lesson the three friends of Job teach us in a remarkable passage from Job 2:11–13:

> When Job's three friends, Eliphaz the Temanite, Bildad the Shuhite and Zophar the Naamathite, heard about all the troubles that had come upon him, they set out from their homes and met together by agreement to go and sympathize with him and comfort him. When they saw him from a distance, they could hardly recognize him; they began to weep aloud, and they tore their robes and sprinkled dust on their heads. Then they sat on the ground with him for seven days and seven nights. No one said a word to him, because they saw how great his suffering was.

Job's friends encouraged him in three ways. They went to him, they shared his pain, and with amazing patience, they sat quietly with him for seven long days. This is encouragement beyond words. The story ended badly because, after seven days, the three friends decided to switch strategies and try to fix Job rather than continue to encourage him. Most of the time, trying to fix an unfixable situation is not encouraging. Remember the power of just being there.

Encourage others with praise. Point them to their strengths, just as

Jesus did. Some may fear to do this, thinking it might feed vanity, but this type of encouragement doesn't swell pride, it conquers doubt. I discovered this truth by accident when I started to encourage my good friend Ben, something which was quite out of character for me at the time. I co-pastor the ROC with Ben. As the senior pastor, Ben does a fantastic job. For some reason, I started to make a point of telling him every Sunday how much I had enjoyed his message.

One Sunday I came up to Ben after the service and told him, "Did you see how everyone quieted down when you spoke? They were soaking in every word." Another Sunday I told him that I had learned a lot from his sermon, that it had blessed me greatly. This new habit was a small thing to do, and I had no idea how significantly it was affecting Ben.

Several months after I started to encourage him, Ben stopped me in the hallway at church. "Rick, I want you to know that six months ago, my wife and I had decided to quit the ministry. I felt discouraged. I didn't have anything to offer anyone. We planned to slowly back out. But then you started to tell me about the impact of my sermons. After a while I started to rethink my earlier decision. Now I want to continue. I can't thank you enough."

I'd had no idea that he had been discouraged or that my words were having such an impact on him. I was surprised that my simple words of encouragement on Sunday mornings had begun to chip away at his despair. But such is the power of encouragement. Encouragement is like the fabled perpetual motion machine—put a little energy in and get a tremendous amount of return out.

Remind people how much God loves them. Point them to the Father, just as Jesus did. That is what we are told to do in Isaiah 35:3–4 (NLT): "Strengthen those who have tired hands, and encourage those who have weak knees. Say to those with fearful hearts, Be strong, and do not fear, for your God is coming.'" I can think of nothing more encouraging in any situation than to be reminded of the power of God. Point those who are hurting to the Psalms. Point those in need of wisdom to Proverbs. Point those who are tired to Jesus Christ, just as he invited us to do in Matthew 11:28: "Come to me, all you who are weary and burdened, and I will give you rest."

Encouragement is a two-way street. Paul understood this when he wrote, "Encourage *one another*" (1 Thessalonians 5:11). I learned this a couple of weeks after I called Brent at the prompting of the Lord to encourage him. It was my turn to need encouragement. I'd had a really bad week, as we all do sometimes. I was feeling discouraged about a couple of projects that I couldn't seem to get off the ground, when Brent called me.

"Rick, this is Brent. I happen to be in the area, and I was wondering if I could stop by and pray over you."

It was my turn to be surprised. "Brent," I said, "I need prayer more than you know. Please come by."

Fifteen minutes later Brent arrived, and we spent a hour praying for God's peace over my household. By the time he left, I was encouraged and lifted up. In Paul's words, I was "strengthened." I had learned that everyone needs encouragement, and everyone can encourage someone else.

Chapter Seven

BE HUMBLE LIKE JESUS WAS HUMBLE

O ne cold, wet Sunday morning, I learned the true meaning of humility from a homeless woman. I was sitting in the back of the
church when I spotted a young woman a few rows ahead of me,
leaning against the wall. She was shivering even though she was bundled
up in her coat. I walked over to her and noticed she had pulled her arms
inside her coat and had pulled it up over her mouth.

She was clearly new to the ROC, so I introduced myself. "Hi, my
name is Rick. Is this your first time here?"

"I'm Ceneta. I'm new to the area, and some people I met on the
streets told me about this church, so I thought I would check it out."

"So you live on the streets?" I asked.

"For the moment, but I hope to find someplace to live soon."

She was still shivering, so I asked, "Would you like a blanket to help
you warm up? I have an extra one downstairs in my car."

"I would love it," she replied. "I am not used to this weather at all."

I ran to my car and got her the blanket. "Thank you," she said as she
wrapped it around her legs.

After the service, I went back to Ceneta. "Is there anything I could
be praying for you?"

She paused for a moment, and then she said something that surprised me so much I assumed I had not heard her correctly. I had expected her to ask God to provide her with a warm place to stay or some
warm, dry clothes. Clearly, she had nothing. It would be perfectly un-
derstandable for her to want some material help. What astonished me
was what she really asked me to pray for.

"I want you to pray that I would be more humble."

Believing that I had misunderstood her, I asked if she wanted me to pray for her *homelessness*.

"No," she said, "I would like you to pray for my *humbleness*."

I prayed for her and told her I would look for her the next Sunday. I never saw her again. I do not know what became of Ceneta. Her prayer request, however, will live with me forever. This was a woman who had nothing in the world, but what she wanted most from God was a humble spirit. She knew something that few people understand. She not only knew the truth of Colossians 3:1–2, she lived it: "Since, then, you have been raised with Christ, set your hearts on things above, where Christ is seated at the right hand of God. Set your minds on things above, not on earthly things."

She had clearly set her mind on the things above, something that might have been easier to do if she possessed some earthly things to begin with! She had nothing, yet she only wanted heavenly qualities. Her story is much like that of Solomon, who, when given the right to ask anything of God, chose to ask for wisdom rather than riches. Not only did she obey the Holy Spirit as he spoke through Paul, she also trusted God's promise: "Humble yourselves, therefore, under God's mighty hand, that he may lift you up in due time" (1 Peter 5:6–7).

That brief encounter taught me more about humility than anything I had ever experienced. I was the one who was humbled by her prayer request.

I'm sure that God was proud of Ceneta. He has always taken delight in the humble. Speaking for God, the prophet Isaiah said, "This is the one I esteem: he who is humble and contrite in spirit" (Isaiah 66:2). David wrote in Psalm 149:4, "For the LORD takes delight in his people; he crowns the humble with salvation."

As with all the universal themes found in the Bible, such as love and forgiveness, humility is a command. Paul wrote in Ephesians 4:2, "Be completely humble and gentle." Besides being commanded, humility has some distinct advantages. It brings forgiveness and healing from God. "If my people, who are called by my name, will humble themselves and pray and seek my face and turn from their wicked ways, then will I hear from heaven and will forgive their sin and will heal their land" (2 Chronicles 7:14). God upholds the humble: "The LORD sustains the humble but casts the wicked to the ground" (Psalm 147:6). God has compassion toward the humble: "He mocks proud mockers but gives grace to the humble" (Proverbs 3:34).

From the beginning of time, God has commanded us to be humble, has delighted in the humble, and has rewarded the humble. Yet, we all seem to struggle with actually *being* humble. Benjamin Franklin observed, in *The Autobiography of Benjamin Franklin,* "In reality there is perhaps not one of our natural passions so hard to subdue as pride. Disguise it, struggle with it, beat it down, stifle it, mortify it as much as one pleases, it is still alive and will every now and then pop out and show itself."

Our problem with humility seems to be the result of a fundamental misunderstanding of what it really means to be humble. Jesus had to teach us how to live a truly humble life.

WHAT DOES IT MEAN TO BE HUMBLE?

Humility is hard to define because it is not just one thing. Every quality of Jesus discussed in this book speaks to his humility. Like the alchemists of old seeking the right mix of ingredients to produce gold, the alchemist of the soul would mix together love, service, forgiveness, trustworthiness, reconciliation, and encouragement to produce humility. Humility can only be understood in light of these other Christlike characteristics.

We have a difficult time putting all these characteristics together into one package. As a result, we define humility in terms of what it is not, rather than what it is. We think of it as denying our accomplishments, when really, it is not exploiting them. We see it as hiding our contributions, when really, it is not promoting them. We see it as the opposite of pride, when really, it is the opposite of arrogance. We consider it to be pretending you are worthless, when really, it is acknowledging the worth of others first. Humility is often viewed as putting yourself down, when its true definition is not putting yourself above others.

Norman Vincent Peale best captured the concept of humility when he wrote in his book *The Power of Ethical Management,* "People with humility don't think less of themselves, they just think about themselves less." The definition of humility, in this context, is simplicity itself: a humble person's focus and attention is on other people. Humble people are thankful for what they have and grateful for what they receive. They expect nothing, though they may deserve much. They don't aspire to greatness, but rather, they seek to serve.

Humility is best measured as the difference between what you deserve and what you are content to receive. If you deserve recognition but are comfortable receiving none, then you are humble. If you think you deserve praise, rightly or wrongly, and are upset when you don't receive it, then you lack humility.

Why Is Humility Difficult?

Humility seems difficult because the world has perverted its meaning. It is touted as a virtue, but in reality, it is one of those rare *unvalued* virtues. We pay lip service to it, but we really don't respect it at all. The word itself has a negative tone. As a verb, "to humble" means to shame, put down, break, crush, debase, degrade, or subdue. As an adjective, its list of synonyms reads like anything but a list of virtues: backward, bashful, fearful, ordinary, self-conscious, self-effacing, servile, sheepish, submissive, timid, unambitious, withdrawn, beggarly, common, insignificant, meager, paltry, petty, pitiful. The list goes on and on, with very few words that would inspire anyone to seek humility in their lives.

Some even consider humility a failing rather than a virtue. Being humble is a weakness. It is even classified as a disease—we equate it with "low self-esteem." As we see it, the humble person cowers in the corner with his head down and shoulders slumped. The humble person allows others to walk all over him and even take credit for what he does.

Is it any wonder we think humility is difficult? How could God take delight in that kind of person? Why would he command us to act like that? The answer is that he doesn't want us to be humble in this perverted sense of the word. This kind of humility is a lie of the enemy. What God wants are confident, bold followers of Christ working in the kingdom with a spirit of humility. While this may seem, by the world's definition, to be contradictory, in God's world, authority, power, confidence, and boldness all coexist with humility. Jesus taught us how this is possible.

HOW JESUS TAUGHT HUMILITY

Jesus often used visual images to describe himself: "I am the gate," "I am the vine," "I am the bread of life," "I am the light of the world." He rarely identified himself with a purely human quality. Humility is one of those rare exceptions. In Matthew 11:29, he said, "I am gentle and humble in heart." This self-description was true of every aspect of his life. From his birth in a barn to his death on a cross, Jesus's life was marked by humility. If the degree of your humility lies in the difference between what you deserve and what you demand, then no one has ever been more humble. No one has ever deserved more yet demanded less. He was holy, yet he lived among sinners. He was a king who accepted the life of a servant. He was rich but possessed nothing. He was a Savior who endured rejection. Each aspect of his life has something to teach us about humility.

HE WAS HOLY YET LIVED AMONG SINNERS

One characteristic of the proud is their contempt for those they consider beneath them. In their arrogance, they refuse to associate with those who do not live up to their standards. Yet Jesus Christ was holy, something even the demons recognized. When Jesus confronted a demon-possessed man, the demon cried out, "I know who you are—the Holy One of God" (Mark 1:24). Hebrews describes Jesus as our High Priest, an office only held by "one who is holy, blameless, pure, set apart from sinners, exalted above the heavens" (Hebrews 7:26). Holiness implies separation from all sin, which means a total rejection of all the ugliness of the world. It is a measure of his humility that Jesus, by virtue of his holiness, had every right to be "set apart from sinners"—yet he chose to live among us.

Some understood his lesson in humility; others were shocked by it. The Pharisees challenged the disciples, "Why does your teacher eat with tax collectors and 'sinners'?" (Matthew 9:11). Trapped in their pride, they could never imagine themselves associating with the people Jesus called friends. Yet the gap between the Pharisees and the hated tax collectors was infinitesimal compared to the gap between our sin and God's holiness.

The first lesson in humility is the same as the first lesson in encouragement: Jesus did not allow his holiness to separate him from others.

He Was a King Who Accepted the Life of a Servant

The proud expect others to acknowledge their position and authority. They desire recognition from others. The humble do not chase after glory; instead, they find joy in the success of others. If anyone had the right to be honored before men, it was Jesus. Revelation 17:14 declares him to be not just *a* king, but "Lord of lords and King of kings." Jesus has always been and always will be the supreme authority, worthy of all our praise and honor. Yet, it is a measure of his humility that he accepted the role of a servant.

Jesus described himself in these terms: "The Son of Man did not come to be served, but to serve" (Matthew 20:28). Paul described him as "taking the very nature of a servant" (Philippians 2:7). Jesus spent his life among the poor and needy. He healed them, taught them, encouraged them, fed them, and listened to them, never demanding praise for his actions.

There is no more poignant story of the servant nature of Jesus than the one found in John 13. On the night he was betrayed, Jesus left the dinner table and washed the feet of the disciples. This was a job reserved for slaves, yet the King of kings took it upon himself. The gap between what he deserved as king and what he accepted as a servant defies human understanding. Such is the mark of humility.

He Was Rich but Possessed Nothing

The proud accumulate things. They take pride in what they own. They expect others to look up to them because they possess the latest, greatest, and most expensive items. They show them off to others and expect the appropriate number of oohs and aahs. The proud find their identity in what they get; the humble find it in what they give.

In reality, none of us really owns anything. Everything belongs to

Jesus. He created the universe and everything in it. When he came to earth, he could have rightly demanded anything he wanted. It is a measure of his humility that he claimed nothing.

I tell the homeless I work with that their lives are actually closer to the life of Jesus than mine. Like them, he was homeless. Like them, he didn't have a job or any source of income. Like them, he relied on others for housing and food. Like them, he was followed and harassed by the authorities of his time. It surprises them to learn that the One who owns everything lived with nothing, just as they do.

Jesus best described his state in Luke 9:58: "Foxes have holes and birds of the air have nests, but the Son of Man has no place to lay his head." This was not a complaint, as a prideful man might voice, but a warning to a man wanting to follow him.

In keeping with his humility, Jesus neither claimed what was his by right nor complained about his lack. Neither did Paul, who modeled the humble life of Jesus. Paul was a rising star in Jerusalem. He was on the fast track to fame, fortune, and power. Then he had an encounter with Jesus on the road to Damascus. As a result of that encounter, he gave up the path to worldly success and followed Jesus. It changed the direction of his life. While Paul never complained, he did tell others about his condition. In one of his letters to the Corinthian church, Paul described himself in a manner that touches the homeless in a special way:

> To this very hour we go hungry and thirsty, we are in rags, we are brutally treated, we are homeless. We work hard with our own hands. When we are cursed, we bless; when we are persecuted, we endure it; when we are slandered, we answer kindly. Up to this moment we have become the scum of the earth, the refuse of the world. (1 Corinthians 4:11–13)

This is the same Paul who wrote in Philippians 4:12, "I have learned the secret of being content in any and every situation, whether well fed or hungry, whether living in plenty or in want." Paul was not humble because he chose to give up a comfortable life for one full of challenges.

He was humble because, like Jesus, he found contentment and peace with what he had.

A Savior Who Was Rejected

The proud long for acceptance. They need others to validate their position, their actions, and their worth. They expect to be thanked when they help someone. They look for approval when they make a decision. They are driven by ambition. They feed off the praise of others. The proud crave rewards from men; the humble seek no reward.

Jesus came to us, giving his life to save us from ourselves, our sin, our folly. It was the ultimate gift that came at a terrible price, yet it is a measure of his humility that, in spite of the gift he brought, he accepted the rejection of men.

There were times when people embraced his message, if not his mission. He was praised and had a following. But there was always an undercurrent of opposition. He was constantly challenged, ridiculed, and rejected. Even in his hometown, he was not received as the Savior, but with offense. The people he had grown up with were hostile to his message, saying, "'Isn't this the carpenter? Isn't this Mary's son and the brother of James, Joseph, Judas and Simon? Aren't his sisters here with us?' And they took offense at him" (Mark 6:3).

Jesus responded to these insults with total humility. He didn't get upset, angry, or discouraged. In effect, he simply said, "Oh well, a prophet is without honor in his own house," and went about his business.

An incident recorded in Luke 17:12–19 illustrates Jesus's humility in the face of rejection. Jesus encountered ten men with leprosy while entering a village. The men cried out to him, asking for mercy. Jesus sent them to the priests, and they were healed. Of the ten, only one returned to both praise God and thank Jesus. Jesus responded, "Were not all ten cleansed? Where are the other nine? Was no one found to return and give praise to God except this foreigner?" (Luke 17:17–18). Jesus, in his humility, was not the least bit concerned that the other nine men did not return to thank him. He was concerned that they did not return to praise his Father.

When the time came for Jesus to face death, even those close to him renounced him. They ran, hid, and when asked about Jesus, denied even knowing him. At the foot of the cross, while Jesus hung dying, the people hurled insults at him. Through it all, he endured the suffering and rejection from the very people he came to save. Remaining humble to the end, Jesus called on the Father to forgive those who scorned him.

HOW CAN WE BE HUMBLE LIKE JESUS?

Jesus taught us a lot about the nature of humility by how he lived. He showed us that it is possible to remain content when you deserve honor and respect but receive only humiliation and rejection. But the most important lesson he taught is that humility is not as the world sees it. Humility does not require us to be self-effacing, sheepish, withdrawn, or fearful, none of which describe Jesus. By his example, humility once again became a virtue and not a weakness. A humble person can be bold and confident without being selfish and vain. Just as pride is not confidence, humility is not self-denial.

There are as many ways to be humble as there are situations that call for humility. The most general indications of humility are seeking the least position and waiting for honor to come to you.

SEEK THE LEAST POSITION

The best example of how humility works, besides the life of Jesus, is found in the parable of the dinner guests. Luke recorded this parable in Luke 14:7–11:

> When he noticed how the guests picked the places of honor at the table, he told them this parable: "When someone invites you to a wedding feast, do not take the place of honor, for a person more distinguished than you may have been invited. If so, the host who invited both of you will come and say to you, 'Give this man your seat.' Then, humiliated, you will have to take the least important place. But when you are invited, take the lowest

place, so that when your host comes, he will say to you, 'Friend, move up to a better place.' Then you will be honored in the presence of all your fellow guests. For everyone who exalts himself will be humbled, and he who humbles himself will be exalted."

In the parable, the humble man does not automatically go to the most important seat because he reasons that someone more worthy is likely to attend. The question is, which seat should the humble man take? If the humble man selects the second most important seat, he faces the same dilemma. What if someone more worthy of the second seat arrives? Then the host will have to ask the humble man to move, thereby humiliating him. Should the humble man select the third most important seat or the fourth? The only way this chain ends is for the humble man to select the least important seat.

In this way, the parable teaches the only logical response of a humble man. To seek anything other than the least seat is to announce that there are people at the wedding of lower status than you are. That is why Jesus told the disciples, "Whoever wants to become great among you must be your servant, and whoever wants to be first must be your slave" (Matthew 20:26–27). Jesus didn't just teach this. He lived it, as Paul noted: "Who, being in very nature God, did not consider equality with God something to be grasped, but made himself nothing, taking the very nature of a servant" (Philippians 2:6–7).

Jesus didn't move from godhood to being the most exalted human on the earth. He didn't move from being the most exalted human on the earth to being a B-list celebrity. Instead, he went to the back of the line. He left himself with nothing. He chose the last seat at the table of humanity. He understood that God was the one who would escort him from the position of servant to his rightful role as King of kings. Joseph went from a slave to the number two man in Egypt, not because he marched into Egypt claiming to be the most intelligent man around, but because he accepted his fate and allowed God to arrange the circumstances that brought him into power.

WAIT FOR OTHERS TO HONOR YOU

Being humble does not mean you will never be honored. In fact, it means the opposite. The humble will be honored in time. This is exactly what Peter wrote in 1 Peter 5:6: "Humble yourselves, therefore, under God's mighty hand, that *he may lift you up* in time." This was also the point of the wedding feast parable. The humble guest will be exalted when he is led from the lowest seat to the seat of honor.

Some might consider that being honored in front of all the guests, as the humble person at the wedding feast would ultimately be, is not a mark of humility. If the person were truly humble, he would not allow himself to be moved to the seat of honor. But the real test of humility is not that you are never honored; it is that you never honor yourself. Jesus made this point while involved in an extended discussion with the Pharisees: "If I glorify myself, my glory means nothing. My Father, whom you claim as your God, is the one who glorifies me" (John 8:54). Just as Jesus did not praise himself but waited for the Father and others to honor him, a humble man will not promote himself but will accept the acclaim of others when it is valid.

If you choose to live like this, your accomplishments will often go unrecognized. Some will consider you weak. Some will try to take advantage of you. In the ultimate irony, some will consider your humility a sneaky way to get others to praise you. One thing is certain: God will honor you for your humility.

Chapter Eight

WALK IN POWER LIKE JESUS WALKED IN POWER

From humility to power may seem like a strange juxtaposition of topics, but it is a natural one in the life of Jesus. I discovered that one Sunday morning at the ROC, and it changed my life forever.

We had prayed off and on for healing after the ROC service for years. Most often our prayers took the form, "Jesus, please heal this person and bring him comfort." There was nothing wrong with these prayers, but they were missing something. Call it authority, boldness, or power, but something wasn't quite complete.

Ben sensed it first, so on a Sunday I will never forget, he stepped up to preach and began with, "I'm tired of praying for healing only to have nothing happen. So from now on, I am going to pray with the expectation that God will heal. I am going to pray with authority because Jesus told us we have authority. Now, is there anyone here today who is sick or is experiencing any pain?"

It was, as usual in the Northwest, a cold, wet Sunday morning. The church was packed. Many were wearing several layers of clothing because, being homeless, they had no place to store extra shirts or coats. They looked tired and disheveled. As Ben's gaze scanned around the church, no one raised his hand. "Come on, someone here must need prayer, and I'm not going on until someone raises their hand."

In the very back row, a young man raised his hand. It was Joe. He had been coming to the ROC off and on for a few months. Ben ran down the aisle to his side. "What do you need prayer for, Joe?" he asked.

Joe explained, "I hurt my right leg a week ago. It's very painful, and I find it difficult to walk."

"Are you in pain right now?"

"Yes."

Ben put one hand on Joe's right leg, raised the other hand into the air, and started to pray. "In the name of Jesus and by his blood shed for us on the cross, I command the pain in this leg to leave Joe right now. I declare that Joe is healed by the authority and power of Jesus."

Then he put his hands down and looked at Joe. "How does your leg feel now?"

"It still hurts."

"Then I will pray again." With force, Ben once again prayed for healing in Joe's leg—and once again, nothing happened. Ben prayed four times that morning, yet Joe's leg was not healed. Ben walked back up to the front. What he said next changed me.

"I will not be defeated. I will not give up. I will continue to pray for Joe for as long as it takes. I will pray for any one of you who needs it until God heals you."

It was like I was hit by a bolt of lightning. Ben was not ruled by fear of failing. He had the faith to believe the promises of Jesus. I decided then and there that I would be as bold as Ben was. Joe's leg might not have been healed that morning, but my faith was.

True to his word, Ben continued to pray with boldness, and three weeks later, a miracle happened. Ben, along with two other members of the ROC leadership team, was sitting at one of the breakfast tables downstairs after church. They were talking to Art, a new member of the ROC. Art was a tall man in his midfifties. He had an air of confidence about him, so Ben was surprised to hear his story.

"I served in Vietnam, and I saw things and did things that haunt me to this day. I can't hold down a job. I have no place to live. I hate everything about my life."

"Can I pray for you? Can I ask God to bring peace to your mind?" Ben asked.

After some thought, Art responded, "I guess so, but I don't deserve anything from God."

So Ben prayed, Art thanked him, and that would have been the end of it if Ben hadn't noticed that as Art stood up to leave, he gripped the edge of the table and slowly lifted himself out of the chair. This prompted Ben to ask, "Art, do you have some problem with your legs or your back?"

Art answered, "My back has hurt for ten years. I am never free of pain."

As Ben put his hand on Art's back, he said, "Let's pray for that." And just as he had done with Joe, in the middle of the breakfast Ben started to pray with authority over Art's back. "Lord, by your name, I command all pain to leave Art's back. I command the muscles to loosen, whatever is out of place to be restored, and all pain to stop. I thank you, Jesus, for the healing you are bringing to Art right now."

Ben looked at Art and asked, "How does your back feel now?"

Art, rubbing his lower back with his left hand, said, "It feels better."

"Okay, try to do something you couldn't do before we prayed."

On cue, Art bent over and touched his toes. He straightened up with a look of shock on his face. "I haven't been able to do that for ten years!" Then he did it again and again. "I can't believe this! I feel so good!"

Ben offered Art a ride to the local shelter, but Art declined, saying, "I want to walk and tell everyone what Jesus just did for me."

Since then, our team has prayed for many people. Some are healed on the spot like Art. Some, like Joe, are not. We don't understand why that happens, but we don't let it stop us either.

Most importantly, I have come to understand something about the model of authority that Jesus taught us.

Jesus, in the midst of his humble life, exercised extraordinary power and authority. He lived in the natural world, but he walked in the supernatural. He did things daily which no one imagined possible. He was like Moses, Elijah, Elisha, and Isaiah all rolled into one. He had authority over demons, the power to heal, the vision to know the future, and the capacity to see into the heart of man. He was defined as much by the miracles he performed as by the wisdom he shared.

It would be easy to say, "Okay, I can be like Jesus in some respects. I can be more loving, more encouraging, more forgiving, less judgmental, and even find more ways to serve others, but miracles? Never. The supernatural? Preposterous." Yet this is precisely where the concept of doing what Jesus would do leads us. Every characteristic of Jesus is more than what the natural world can sustain. From the quality of his forgiveness to the depth of his love, Jesus never did anything in a small way. Empowered by the Holy Spirit, he lived and breathed the supernatural. Such is the nature of the kingdom of God, just as Paul told the Corinthian church: "For the kingdom of God is not a matter of talk but of power" (1 Corinthians 4:20). The Greek word Paul uses for "power" means "miraculous power." This stands in stark contrast to modern-day religion, which is all about talk and very little about power.

It is time to confront what Jesus really meant when he said we would not only do everything he did, but more. It's time you discover the power of the Holy Spirit within you. It's time to acknowledge the "new creature" you have become.

What Is Power?

Power is easy to define. It is the ability to control our environment. In the natural world, power is constrained by the laws of physics and the laws of man. The most powerful man in the United States is still constrained by our laws. Even though a dictator makes the laws and can violate them at will, he is still limited: such a dictator could order the execution of an innocent man, but he does not have the power to undo the sentence once it has been carried out.

In God's world, however, power knows no bounds. When Jesus said "All things are possible with God" (Mark 10:27), it was the ultimate expression of power. The words "all things" mean exactly what they appear to mean—all, any, every, the whole. Nothing is excluded, nor are "all things" limited by the laws of science. In the kingdom of God, power is total, absolute, supreme. If God wills it, it happens.

When power of this magnitude is exercised on earth, we have but one name for it—miracle. A miracle is something that, by all normal standards, is impossible and unexplainable. This is the kind of power Jesus exercised on earth. This is the kind of power we are called to use as disciples of Jesus. C.S. Lewis wrote in his book *Miracles*, "The mind which asks for a non-miraculous Christianity is a mind in the process of relapsing from Christianity into mere 'religion.'" I tell the homeless at the ROC that they have more power in their little fingers than the president of the US because they believe in Jesus.

How Did Jesus Display Power?

From his first miracle of changing water into wine to his resurrection from the dead, Jesus walked in power. He demonstrated his power over the physical elements when he calmed the storm. Countless times, he shocked the Pharisees and others when he exposed their innermost thoughts. He healed the lame, the blind, and the leper. He raised people from the dead. He walked on water. He cast out demons. At his command, a fig tree withered. He turned a few loaves of bread and two small fish into a meal for more than five thousand. He restored a severed ear. He had detailed knowledge of future events. He clearly demonstrated that with him, as with his Father, nothing was impossible.

Even before Jesus started his ministry, the enemy knew the extent of his power. At the first temptation in the wilderness, Satan knew Jesus had the power to change the stones into bread. Satan was right. Jesus could have exercised power at that moment, but he didn't. Miracles were an important part of his ministry, but they were not to be done at the suggestion of the enemy.

The purpose of miracles has always been to reveal God. Ever since Moses confronted Pharaoh, God has used miracles to identify himself and establish his authority. Nothing changed when Jesus came, as he explained, "The miracles I do in my Father's name speak for me" (John 10:25).

Miracles were an important part of the process of building trust and belief in the people he touched. Jesus told a crowd, "Even though you do not believe me, believe the miracles, that you may know and understand that the Father is in me, and I in the Father" (John 10:38). Nicodemus, one of the Pharisees, got the point. He told Jesus, "Rabbi, we know you are a teacher who has come from God. For no one could perform the miraculous signs you are doing if God were not with him" (John 3:2). The flip side of what Nicodemus understood is that if God is with someone, that person can perform miracles.

The apostle John explained that the reason miracles were reported was to validate Jesus: "Jesus did many other miraculous signs in the presence of his disciples, which are not recorded in this book. But these are written that you may believe that Jesus is the Christ, the Son of God, and that by believing you may have life in his name" (John 20:30–31).

While the primary motivation of miracles was to testify to the truth of who he was, Jesus also performed miracles out of a strong sense of compassion for those in need. Jesus healed the leper because he was "filled with compassion" (Mark 1:40–41). Jesus fed the five thousand because, "I have compassion for these people, they have already been with me three days and have nothing to eat" (Matthew 15:32). Matthew 14:14 describes the typical response of Jesus to crowds: "When Jesus landed and saw a large crowd, *he had compassion on them* and healed their sick."

In the face of questioning, Jesus performed miracles to validate his message. In the presence of great need, he performed miracles out of compassion. Both motives worked together in almost all of the miracles Jesus performed. Both achieved their purpose. God was revealed, and people were helped.

Perhaps the issue is not whether Jesus performed miracles, but how he performed them. Did he perform them as God, relying on the same power he used to create the universe? Or did he do them as a man, filled with the Holy Spirit, calling on the power of the Spirit? The answer is important because if he did them as God, we have no hope of following his example. If he did them as a man, then we can do them as well.

The answer is clear. Paul told us that Jesus totally emptied himself of his godhood and "made himself nothing, taking the very nature of a servant, being made in human likeness" (Philippians 1:7). When the Jews challenged Jesus, arguing that he was claiming equality with God by his actions, he replied, "I tell you the truth, the Son can do nothing by himself" (John 5:19). Jesus performed miracles, but not as God. He did them as a man filled with the Holy Spirit. That is why, after he left,

Peter, Paul, Stephen, Barnabas, and countless others continued to perform miracles. That is why all of us can do what Jesus did, even to the point of performing miracles.

YOU CAN WALK IN POWER

You have become a new creature. That new creature is the very image of Jesus Christ, just as Paul told the Colossians: "You have taken off your old self with its practices and have put on the new self, which is being renewed in knowledge in the image of its Creator" (Colossians 3:9–10). The word used for "image" is better translated "likeness." As that new creature, as a likeness of Christ, you can do what Jesus did, including miracles.

Jesus said believers would be able to do what he did. And there are plenty of other passages that make the same case. Jesus promised the disciples that miraculous power would come upon them when they received the Holy Spirit: "I am going to send you what my Father has promised; but stay in the city until you have been clothed with *power* from on high" (Luke 10:49). Paul recognized the power he had received and wrote about it in 1 Corinthians 2:4: "My message and my preaching were not with wise and persuasive words, but with a demonstration of the Spirit's power." Later, Paul told Timothy that power had been shared with him: "For God did not give us a spirit of timidity, but a spirit of power" (1 Timothy 1:7).

Some in the church today argue that we don't have this power because it was only given to the apostles. When they died, miracles died with them. If that were true and only Jesus and the apostles *could* perform miracles, then only Jesus and the apostles *would* have performed miracles. But that was not the case. Stephen was not an apostle, yet he performed "great wonders and miraculous signs among the people" (Acts 6:8). Barnabas, also not an apostle, was credited with performing signs and wonders as well (Acts 15:12). When Jesus sent out the seventy-two as recorded in Luke 10, none of whom were apostles, they performed miracles. Clearly, God's power through the Holy Spirit was never limited to the eleven original apostles and Paul.

Still uncomfortable with the idea that ordinary believers can perform miracles today, others in the church take the position that miracles did not die out with the apostles but with the early church. They argue that once the church no longer needed miracles, God withdrew the authority to perform them. But their argument falls apart when we remember that the purpose of miracles in the time of Jesus was to validate the gospel and display God's compassion to the needy. Both are needed today as much as they were in the first-century church. In fact, considering the nature of the world today, perhaps miracles are needed today more than ever! Besides, why would God suddenly change his approach and leave us without one of the weapons that had worked so well against the enemy for centuries? Are we to believe that the book of Acts was just a tease? That for some reason God said, "Here is what you could have done if you lived in the time of the early church, but not anymore"? Why would God lay the foundation for a church full of power and authority, working miracles, and then strip it all away?

Paul wrote about the composition of the church in an important passage found in 1 Corinthians 12:27–28:

Now you are the body of Christ, and each one of you is a part of it. And in the church God has appointed first of all apostles, second prophets, third teachers, then workers of miracles, also those having gifts of healing, those able to help others, those with gifts of administration, and those speaking in different kinds of tongues.

Paul said these were the building blocks of the church, the parts of the body of Christ on earth. What happened? Did God dismantle the church and dismember the body of Christ? Did he say, "You can keep teachers, helpers, and administrators, but no healers, miracle workers, or prophets"? What kind of sense does that make?

Nowhere in the Bible does it say to expect power to be withdrawn at any moment. Actually, Jesus told us that the power of the Holy Spirit that fell upon the apostles and the early church at Pentecost would remain until the Great Commission was completed: "But you will receive power when the Holy Spirit comes on you; and you will be my witnesses in Jerusalem, and in all Judea and Samaria, and to the ends of the earth" (Acts 1:8). The phrase "the ends of the earth" means the uttermost, farthest, final place on earth. This is far from being completed today. The power of the Holy Spirit is still needed to fulfill the command Jesus gave just before he ascended into heaven.

You, as a new creature in Christ, have the same power given to the apostles and the early church because you are charged with the same task of being his witness to the final places on earth. Yet, if we are honest, most of us are not operating in this power today. If the purpose of the Holy Spirit was to bring power, then either we don't have the Holy Spirit filling us anymore and we have to ask why, or we *do* have the Holy Spirit filling us with power and we have to ask why we aren't walking in it.

You have spiritual gifts that allow you to do things that defy the natural world. You can encourage the discouraged, comfort the oppressed, heal the sick, feed the hungry, pray for the lost, preach to the masses, bring peace to the afflicted, and prophesy to those who need wisdom. You can do all this with the same power that Jesus relied on when he walked the earth.

For years, I was one of those who believed that miracles were no longer a part of the church. My walk with God was limited to reading the Bible, Sunday worship, serving others in the church, and prayer. There is nothing wrong with any of those things, but the limitation meant that I was not really doing what Jesus did. Instead, I was doing what I could do in my own strength. My actions weren't enough, but I didn't know that. I occasionally heard about miracles, but I dismissed them as unfounded rumors, Christian legends, or worse, fakes. Until I saw one happen right in front of me, just like Ben did when Art was healed.

It happened one morning after the church service at the ROC. As always, we asked anyone who needed prayer to stay after the service. Even though I did not believe in miracles, I still prayed that God would heal the sick because, well, that's what Christians do. I had done it for more than twenty-five years. This morning, however, the result of that prayer was to be very different.

At the end of the service, a homeless woman named Claire got up from her seat and struggled to move to the front. She grimaced in obvious pain as she used the chairs to support herself. She explained that she was having a painful attack of gout and could barely walk. I placed my hand on her shoulder, and along with one of our other leaders, Matilda, I started to pray. This time, instead of asking God to heal Claire, we commanded the pain to leave in the name of Jesus. We commanded her legs to heal. All of a sudden, I noticed my hand heat up. At about that same time, Claire let out a cry. "Whoa, what was that?"

"What happened?" I asked.

"A warmth spread from my shoulder down to the bottom of my feet," she said.

"How do your legs feel now?"

She paused for a moment to think about my question. Her attention had focused so much on the calming warmth engulfing her body that she hadn't thought about the pain at all.

"The pain in my left leg is completely gone," she said. "My right leg still feels a little bit of pain."

While she did not leap on her way out of the room, she walked out at a normal pace, without requiring the help of the chairs. Ben met her at the door and noticed she was crying. Not knowing what had just happened, he asked, "Why the tears?" Her answer was remarkable. She was not crying because she had been healed. Rather, she told Ben that she "had just been touched by God."

This was the first time I prayed for a person who was instantly healed. It was Claire's time to be touched by God, and it was my moment of transition. I now had a firsthand experience with the power of the Holy Spirit. Since then, I have seen many more miracles, including feeling a woman's left leg grow in my hands to match the length of her right leg, having several cancerous tumors melt away, and watching years of pain disappear, and just as it is described in the Bible, I have seen the lame walk again. Not everyone I pray for is healed, but it only has to happen once for us to realize that we are capable of walking in power just as Jesus did.

You are a new creature formed in the likeness of Jesus Christ, filled with the Holy Spirit, able to do what he did. Start walking in that identity. Start exercising power.

It is not easy. You will be opposed. Heidi Baker, a missionary in Mozembique, felt like she had a calling to heal the blind. She prayed for thirteen blind people with no healing, but when she prayed for the fourteenth blind person, she saw the woman's eyes change as she was healed. You need to exercise that kind of perseverance.

Power may not come in the form of healing for you, but it will come. Be like Peter who brazenly stepped out of the boat, and if only for a short time, walked on water.

Epilogue

This book is about an outrageous, unimaginable, impossible goal: to walk the earth as Jesus Christ did. If Jesus himself had not declared it possible in John 14:12, it would be sacrilegious to even consider it. I had a pastor once tell me that it is wrong to build a whole theology on just one verse. He was right. On the other hand, it is equally wrong to take a single verse that makes us uncomfortable or that we find unbelievable and ignore it. If I did that, I would slowly chip away at the Bible, one uncomfortable verse at a time, until I had nothing left except perhaps John 3:16.

Besides, this goal is based on far more than what Jesus said in John 14:12. Paul said we could be imitators of Christ as well—so did Peter and the writer of Hebrews. And in the end, every aspect of the life of Jesus covered in this book is a command. We are not *asked* to do what Jesus did, we are *told* to do what Jesus did. It appears that the Ten Commandments which describe how we should behave have been replaced by the Seven Commandments which proscribe who we should be: the image of Jesus Christ. John 14:12 is just the assurance we need that it is possible. If Jesus takes over your life, if you are totally surrendered to him, if he is in control, how then do you think you will live?

If this book has accomplished its purpose, it should have gone far beyond encouraging you to do what Jesus did. It really is designed with three goals in mind:

- To introduce you to the new creature you have become
- To introduce you to the man Jesus was
- To allow you to introduce others to Jesus

In many ways, once you accept the truth of the premise that you can do what Jesus did, you will find it makes sense. Jesus came to do more than just die for us. He came to show us how to live as the redeemed. For his sacrifice to make any sense to those of us waiting for his return, our lives must be transformed. What better, more meaningful way can we be transformed than into the image of Christ?

In the process of becoming more like Christ, we also begin to understand who he was. It is my hope that this book has been your introduction to the fullness of Jesus, your opportunity to meet Jesus as:

- A man of unceasing prayer
- A man of unconditional love
- A man of sacrificial service
- A man of boundless forgiveness
- A man who never judged
- A man full of encouragement
- A man of genuine humility
- A man of infinite power

This is the Man we are called to imitate. This is our role model for life. This is the Man that Paul wrote so emphatically about, using the strongest words possible to drive his point home: "So I tell you this, and *insist on it in the Lord,* that you must no longer live as the Gentiles do… [but] put on the new self, created to be like God in true righteousness and holiness" (Ephesians 4:17, 24).

A song by David Will called "You're the Only Jesus," best captures the intent of this book. The song challenges me, much as I hope this book has challenged you, to understand that you are truly the only Jesus others will ever encounter.

Before I realized the truths in this book, whenever I heard that song, I always thought, *What a nice sentiment; I should be a good person.* Now I understand that the call is so much deeper than that. I must do what Jesus did precisely because I may very well be "the only Jesus some will ever see." It is a challenge, but we are all up to it. It will not be easy, but it will be an adventure. If you do everything Jesus did and more, you can expect the same reception Jesus got and worse. Yet, no matter what the immediate outcome, the end is assured. You will one day face Jesus and hear the words we all long to hear: "Well done, good and faithful servant."

ACKNOWLEDGMENTS

I have to once again acknowledge the six people to which this book is dedicated: Brian Brent, Bonnie Spillman, Michelle Sweem, Brent Eriksen, Jon Graciano, and Ben Windham. While they had nothing to do with the writing of this book, they had everything to do with its contents. In many ways they were my models of how someone can do what Jesus did.

I also want to acknowledge the fine people at Deep River Books, especially Kit Tosello, who led me through the whole process, and Rachel Starr Thomson, who did an excellent job editing the work.

References

Baker, Heidi. *Compelled by Love.* Lake Mary, FL: Charisma House, 2008.

Lewis, C.S. *Miracles.* New York: HarperOne, 2001.

Spurgeon, Charles. *The Check Book of the Book of Faith.* New York: Christian Heritage, 2005.

Stark, Dr. Rodney. *What Americans Really Believe.* Waco, TX: Baylor University Press, 2008.

Additional Resources

If you are interested in following up on the process of adopting Jesus Christ as your role model, there is a workbook available titled *30 Days of Doing What Jesus Did* available from the author's website:

www.thekingdomisnear.com

Dr. Spillman is also available to teach a six-hour course (in one day or spread over two or three days).

Contact him at:

thekingdomisnear@gmail.com